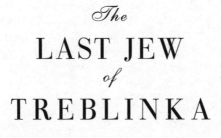

The
LAST JEW
of
TREBLINKA

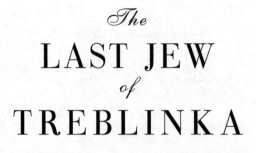

The
LAST JEW
of
TREBLINKA

A Survivor's Memory
1942–1943

CHIL RAJCHMAN

Translated from the Yiddish by
Solon Beinfeld

PEGASUS BOOKS
NEW YORK

THE LAST JEW OF TREBLINKA

Pegasus Books LLC
80 Broad Street, 5th Floor
New York, NY 10004

First published in Great Britain in 2010 by
MacLehose Press
an imprint of Quercus
21 Bloomsbury Square
London WC1A 2NS

First Pegasus Books cloth edition February 2011
First Pegasus Books trade paperback edition 2012

ISBN: 978-1-60598-342-4

10 9 8 7 6 5 4

Printed in the United States of America
Distributed by W. W. Norton & Company, Inc.
www.pegasusbooks.us

For all those to whom it was not possible to tell this tale.

Andrés, Daniel, José Rajchman

"It is the writer's duty to tell the terrible truth,
and it is a reader's civic duty to learn this truth.
To turn away, to close one's eyes and walk past
is to insult the memory of those who have perished."

VASILY GROSSMAN

The time had passed when each new day was bright,
precious and unique: the future stood before us,
grey amd shapeless, like an impenetrable barrier.
For us, history had stopped.

PRIMO LEVI

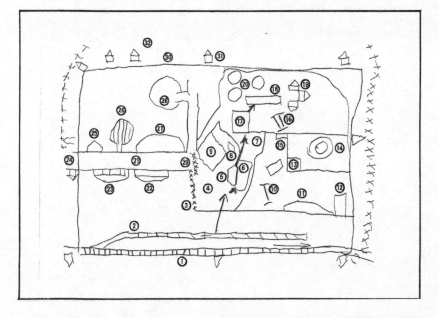

MAP DRAWN BY VASILY GROSSMAN IN SEPTEMBER 1944 WHILE WRITING "THE HELL OF TREBLINKA"

① RAILWAY LINE

② BRANCH LINE CONSTRUCTED BY GERMANS

③ BARBED-WIRE FENCE 6 METRES HIGH

④ ROLL CALL SQUARE

⑤ UNDRESSING

⑥ WOMEN'S "HAIRDRESSERS"

⑦ "ROAD OF NO RETURN"

⑧ LATRINE

⑨ BARRACKS FOR JEWISH WORKERS, 700 MEN

⑩ RECEPTION CAMP (LOWER CAMP)

⑪ CLOTHES STORE

⑫ SHOE STORE

⑬ "DOCTOR'S HUT"

⑭ "LAZARET"

⑮ LATRINE

⑯ DEATH CAMP (UPPER CAMP)

⑰ "BATH HOUSE"

⑱ GRILL

⑲ BARRACKS FOR 300 JEWISH WORKERS

⑳ GRAVE PITS

㉑ ROAD

㉒ ARSENAL

㉓ BARRACKS FOR GERMAN STORES

㉔ GUARD HOUSE, 1 GERMAN, 5 UKRAINIANS

㉕ ADMINISTRATION BUILDING

㉖ "UKRAINIANS'" BARRACKS

㉗ BAKERY, DOCTOR, DENTIST, BARBER FOR GERMANS

㉘ ZOO

㉙ BARBED-WIRE FENCE 3 METRES HIGH

㉚ BARBED WIRE, PINE BRANCHES, BLANKETS, 3 METRES HIGH

㉛ WATCH TOWER, GUARD WITH MACHINE GUN

㉜ ANTI-TANK BARRIER

THE BLACK ARROWS INDICATE THE PATH FOLLOWED BY A NEW TRANSPORT OF JEWS FROM ARRIVAL AT THE "STATION", THROUGH

THE UNDRESSING AREAS AND DOWN "THE ROAD OF NO RETURN" TO THE GAS CHAMBERS –

AND THEN THE GRILLS ON WHICH THE CORPSES WERE BURNED.

Preface

BY SAMUEL MOYN

IN MID-APRIL 1945, AMERICAN GIs LIBERATED
Buchenwald, while British soldiers marched, horrified,
into Bergen-Belsen. There they found scenes of unimagi-
nable suffering, men of bones and skin somehow standing
on spindly legs, amidst piles of emaciated corpses. Celebrated
journalists documented what must have seemed the nether
pole of human depravity: the worst an inhuman regime could
achieve. Even as thousands of typhus-stricken survivors died,
witnesses to a liberation that came too late for them, Margaret
Bourke-White took chilling photographs that captured the
consequences of the Nazi designs, and a picture of evil was
set. And yet, Treblinka was absent from this picture.

Chil Rajchman's memoir of that place lay in Yiddish
manuscript for decades, and the very name "Treblinka"

became widely known only decades after war's end. Yet Rajchman was witness to a very different reality, at a site that—unlike the concentration camps—Nazis had long since tried to wipe from the map. It was further east, in the territories the Red Army liberated, and where far more pitiless dynamics of killing were unleashed than the global audience of Belsen and Buchenwald could have imagined. The Nazi project of extermination reached its most terrible extremity in Treblinka and at the other industrial killing centers whose names were at first equally unfamiliar.

These were places very different than the Western concentration camps, which became lethal only in the last months of a war, as a failed regime lost its ability to feed its prisoners. In the eastern killing facilities, by contrast, the Nazi state did what it set out to do, after it chose the final solution of extermination. Unlike in the West, the victims in the east were dealt immediate extinction on arrival, and died as Jews targeted as Jews by the regime. Next to no one survived: compared to the scores of memoirs testifying to the concentrations camps, which though terrible were generally not intended to kill, a paltry number could write of any experiences in the death camps. Only those few who, like Rajchman, were selected to operate the machinery of extinction in the *Sonderkommando* of the killing center, and not put to death themselves along the way or at the end, could tell what happened.

Along with a handful of other documents, Rajchman's astonishing memoir—drafted mostly in hiding before the Soviets reached Warsaw, where he had fled after his unlikely survival and escape—is one of the best descriptions of the

Nazi project of extermination at its most spare and deadly. Indeed, the era can be known in its true horror only thanks to texts like this one.

IN CONTRAST TO THE WESTERN CONCENTRATION CAMPS, which originated before World War II for a variety of Adolf Hitler's internal enemies—communists and criminals were their main residents until the war and indeed during much of it—the extermination camps of the east arose in the heat of conflict on the eastern front. In the second half of 1941 the process of exterminating the Jews slowly shifted. Dominated immediately after the German invasion of the Soviet Union by mass shootings beyond the Molotov-Ribbentrop line, it now turned into a policy of constructing death factories behind it, as the triumphs of the invasion of the east in Operation Barbarossa slowed and a lightning victory came to seem out of reach.

Following Heinrich Himmler's orders, the SS began by setting up Chełmno, in the Wartheland district of Greater Germany, and then Bełżec and Sobibór, across the border in the "General Government," as the Nazis called their new colony made up of former Polish territories. Then Himmler ordered the erection of a new site, closer to Warsaw, also part of the General Government, and its largest city. Situated some fifty miles northeast of the city, on the Bug River, Treblinka was complete in June 1942. It became the centerpiece of "Operation Reinhard," as the project of exterminating the Jews of the General Government came to be known, in honor of Reinhard Heydrich, a lieutenant of Himmler's who was assassinated that spring. In the end, 1.3 million Jews were killed as part of this policy, nearly 800,000 of them at Treblinka, in not much more than a year.

As if his destiny of living through so much death cuts him off from his prior existence, Rajchman tells nothing of his life before the "grim railway cars" bear him to this place in the memoir's opening lines. But more information is available in testimonies he later recorded for the United States Holocaust Memorial Museum in 1988, and the USC Shoah Foundation Institute in 1994. Born Yechiel Meyer Rajchman—Chil for short—on June 14, 1914, in Łódź, he fled east with a sister as the Germans invaded in 1939. Two years later, when with the Soviet campaign the final solution began in earnest, Rajchman found himself in the vicinity of Lublin, from where he was deported to Treblinka in the roundups that were intended erase a millennial Jewish presence from the area.

Arrival there means the immediate loss of his sister, along with all other women and children: the only work for which selection is possible at a death camp is for the handful of men needed to run the camp itself. Across the Molotov-Ribbentrop line, where hundreds of thousands of Jews were shot, mobile killing units took on the job of extermination; at Treblinka, as at the other death facilities, the logistics of destruction called for only a few dozen SS, some more Ukrainian assistants, and the Jews themselves. Rajchman refers his killers, indiscriminately, as "murderers," with only a few singled out by name or nickname, notably Kurt Franz, "the doll," famous for his dog, his vanity, and his cruelty. Rajchman knows the cremation specialist summoned for his expertise, almost certainly Herbert Floss, simply as "the artist." And in passing, he mentions Ivan, dubbed "the terrible," a sadistic brute whom Rajchman later believed he recognized in Ivan Demjanjuk, at whose American trial he testified.

RAJCHMAN'S MEMOIR IS ABOVE ALL ELSE AN INCISIVE depiction of how the Nazis organized the destruction of millions of human beings and, indeed, reorganized and refined the process as time went on. As a worker, he moves from Treblinka 1 to Treblinka 2, sections of the killing center compartmentalized from each other by the gas chambers, to which arriving Jews are led along the *Schlauch* or corridor that the Germans euphemistically dubbed the "road to heaven." Rajchman avoids that route somehow, and observes how man-made mass death is put into motion. If he knows on arrival what this place is—poignantly telling his sister not to bother with their bags on the train—he learns the details of its "professional" evil only through harsh experience.

In brief, succeeding chapters, Rajchman tells of the infernal division of labor, through which the steps in the process of extermination are carefully apportioned, and whose shifting roles allow him to survive. He begins as a barber, shearing women's hair prior to their gassing, a fate many of the women he encounters clearly foresee, in one of the most affecting scenes Rajchman portrays in the narrative. Transferred to the secretive other zone of the camp, he carries bodies, asphyxiated by carbon monoxide generated from a diesel motor, often transformed beyond recognition, intertwined with one another, and repulsively swollen. Later, and for most of his time, Rajchman is made a so-called "dentist," part of the crew of Jews charged with extracting gold from the teeth of corpses and searching the bodies for hidden valuables.

If the "work" evolves as Polish Jewry meets its end, it is because the Nazis sought a way to eliminate the evidence of their deeds. They order thousands of corpses dug up for burning, after a policy change alters the method of disposal from burial to cremation. In the early days, the Jews are told to layer sand over the tombs carefully, but—as if in a sickening act of posthumous resistance—the blood of the Jews is "unable to rest," and "thrusts itself upwards to the surface." After an era of crude and unsuccessful bonfires is initiated, the "artist" arrives and teaches them how to do it. The task is massive, as the formerly interred corpses have to be set aflame along with newly killed bodies, for a time in the hundreds of thousands per month. Women, Floss instructs, burn better; placed at the base, they are the torches that will consume the rest. But there are still fragments of bones that the Nazis make the Jews painstakingly collect, often thwarting their hopes of leaving some trace—anything—to be discovered by future generations of this infamy.

Inside the camp, a tenuous solidarity rules, even as the unbearable circumstances push many *Sonderkommando* members to suicide. For others, plans for escape and, eventually, the extraordinary insurrection of August 2, 1943 germinate. From the day Rajchman arrives to the fateful day he revolts and escapes, physical depredations are omnipresent. Hunger is constant, and illness a frightening threat. The beatings and whippings Rajchman and others repeatedly suffer are understood as dangerous for their potential consequences. A cut face means certain death: the SS kill those with such visible wounds. Injury that interferes with helping the Nazis kill other Jews—the only reason Rajchman and others at Treblinka are allowed to live—is repaid by execution. He is fortunate that a fellow inmate can treat his suppurating gash with impromptu surgery before the guards see its severity. Throughout *The Last Jew*, the prose is factual, made all the more devastating for its exquisitely controlled rage at the crimes he is describing. By the end, his anger has already crystallized in resistance and flight for the sake of life and memory.

WOULD IT HAVE MADE A DIFFERENCE HAD RAJCHMAN'S memories come to light right away? Perhaps not. Yankel Wiernik, whom Rajchman mentions, published his story of a year in Treblinka in Polish in 1944; it was translated into a number of other languages thereafter, but not many noticed. Other memoirists, notably Richard Glazar and Shmuel Willenberg, eventually published their testimonies. Their grim tasks mostly accomplished, the death camps, including Treblinka, were razed; only Majdanek, which like Auschwitz combined labor and extermination, survived long enough to by liberated by the Soviets, who publicized their findings as assaults on humanity. Vasily Grossman, the brilliant Soviet Jewish writer, visited Treblinka after the Red Army arrived in summer 1944, and on the basis of few sources, drafted and published an exceptionally powerful description that fall. A number of survivors, including Rajchman, testified before a postwar Polish historical commission, and Rachel Auerbach synthesized what was known in Yiddish soon after (she later became a leading figure at Israel's Yad Vashem memorial).

Yet even though it was easier to grasp them there compared to the West, the true purposes of the death camps were not helpful information in the Soviet Union, or in the lands of Eastern Europe where the Red Army finally put Hitler down. Even for Grossman, in 1944, the Jewish identity of Treblinka's victims is clearly registered, but not emphasized. And by a year later, when in collaboration with Ilya Ehrenburg Grossman finished a *Black Book* detailing Nazi crimes against Jews, and sought to reincorporate his Treblinka essay, the Soviets could not accept the realities of predominantly Jewish victimhood. Though Grossman's essay had circulated on its own (and had been translated into French), the plates of the *Black Book* were destroyed. Whether in the west, where Belsen and Buchenwald were so prominent, or the east, where it was "humanity" not Jewry above all that suffered, no one else could allow themselves to see what Rajchman and his fellow survivors of the Treblinka revolt did. What the Nazis did to Jews as Jews at these killing centers—exterminate them in millions on arrival—did not easily serve existing agendas at the time.

Having been constructed as a concentration camp in 1940, Auschwitz, west of the General Government, surged as a death facility as Treblinka had done its work. It killed mainly Jews and others from beyond Poland, including Hungarian Jewry in a paroxysm in 1944; but because its main components interned many sorts of people, and many Jews as workers, its survivors were by an enormous measure witnesses to a western-style concentration experience rather than an eastern-style death factory. By many of its more than 100,000 survivors (many of whom were not Jews), in immediate Soviet publicity, and even at the Nuremberg trials, Auschwitz was presented as a concentration camp. Its Birkenau site, a Treblinka but one confusingly embedded in a universe of internment and labor, was given shorter shrift for a long time. The death camps became known only later, as the wheels of justice began to grind, and Holocaust memory coalesced decades after the fact.

RAJCHMAN'S ESCAPE LEADS ONLY TO NEW TRAVAILS, including a moving portrait of flight in the countryside, in which the human kindness and unconscionable collaboration of local Polish peasants are both on display. He barely mentions it, but Rajchman lived through the 1944 Warsaw uprising against the Nazis, and ultimately—after the Soviet liberation of the city in January 1945—migrated to Uruguay, where he lived a productive life in the business world and had three sons. After some obvious additions after wartime to this crucial documentation (certainly the final few paragraphs), and possible revisions, a friend of Rajchman's family agitated for its publication. As fate would have it, this work is posthumous: Rajchman died in 2004.

That Rajchman bore witness to Treblinka's horrors and that his memoir has belatedly appeared is a gift, but it is a bleak and discomfiting testament, not a redemptive and uplifting one. Even the Treblinka revolt, often treated as an uncomplicated triumph of the human spirit, is narrated by this participant in tones that are far from straightforwardly heroic. Rajchman bore witness, but did not offer lessons: the memoir's insights seem to be for a posterity that still does not know where they should lead.

Through the unprecedented landscape of his text, Rajchman's proofs of how far beyond the boundaries of the imaginable humans can go in their treatment of one another are piled more obscenely than the mountains of corpses the Nazis put to the torch. In the end, its list of abominations seems to offer too many faces of evil to decide easily what was most atrocious in this place and time.

But my choice, I think, is Rajchman's disturbing reflection—offered in passing, but all the more upsetting for that reason—that it was better for him to lose his mother when he was a child than for her to live long enough to descend into the hell she would never have escaped. It is a dismal testament to their destruction of the ordinary moral world that the Nazis could make one of the worst imaginable events of any life seem like it had been a fortunate event.

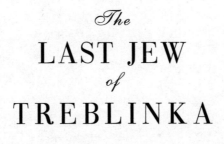

The
LAST JEW
of
TREBLINKA

Chapter One

❦

*In sealed railway cars to
an unknown destination*

THE GRIM RAILWAY CARS CARRY ME THERE, TO THAT place. They transport from all directions: from east and west, from north and south. By day and by night. In all seasons of the year people are brought there: spring and summer, autumn and winter. The transports travel there without hindrance and without limit, and Treblinka grows richer in blood day by day. The more people who are brought there, the more Treblinka is able to receive them.

I, like all the others, do not know where and for what reason we are travelling. We try, nevertheless, insofar as possible, to find out something about our journey. The Ukrainian robbers who guard us will not do us the favour of replying. The only thing we hear from them is—Hand over gold, hand over money and valuables! These criminals

3

visit us constantly. Almost every hour another one of them terrorizes us. They beat us mercilessly with their rifle butts, and each of us tries as best he can to shut the murderers up with a few zlotys in order to avoid their blows. That is what our journey is like.

We travel from Lubartow station, some 20 kilometres from Lublin. I travel with my pretty young sister Rivka, nineteen years old, and a good friend of mine, Wolf Ber Rojzman, and his wife and two children. Almost all of those in the car are my close acquaintances, from the same small town, Ostrow Lubelski. There are about 140 of us in the car. It is extraordinarily tight, with dense, stale air, all of us pressed against one another. Despite the fact that men and women are all together, each of us, in these crowded conditions, has to perform his natural functions on the spot where he is standing . . . From all corners one hears deep groans, and people ask each other—Where are we going? Everyone shrugs and replies with a deep *oy*. No-one knows where the road leads, and at the same time no-one wants to believe that we are going where our sisters and brothers, our nearest and dearest, have been sent over a period of many months.

Sitting near me is my friend Katz, an engineer by profession. He assures me that we are going to Ukraine and that we will be able to settle in the countryside there and work the land. He explains that he knows this for certain because that is what he was told by a German lieutenant, the manager of a state farm in Jedlanka, 7 kilometres from our little town. The German told Katz this ostensibly as a friend, since Katz had from time to time repaired an electric motor for him. I want to believe it, though I know it is in fact not so.

We travel. The train stops often because of the signals, since it is running outside the timetable and therefore has to wait and let the normal trains through. We travel through various stations, among them Lukow and Siedlice. At every opportunity, when the train stops, I beg the Ukrainians, who descend to the platform, to bring us a little water. They do not reply, but if you give them a gold watch, they hand you a sip of water. Many of my friends give them their valuables but do not receive the promised water. I am an exception. I ask a Ukrainian for a little water. He demands 100 zlotys from me for a bottle of water. I agree. In a short while he brings me a half-litre bottle of water. I ask him how long we will be travelling. His reply is—Three days, because we are going to Ukraine. I begin to think maybe it's really true . . . We have been travelling for nearly fifteen hours, though the distance is about 120 kilometres.

It is 4:00 in the morning as we approach a station called Treblinka, which lies some 7 kilometres from Malkinia. We stop. The cars are sealed and we don't know what will happen to us. We wait for the train to move again. My sister tells me she is hungry. But we have little in the way of food. Leaving our town unexpectedly, it was impossible to procure supplies. The same was true in the town of Lubartow. I explain to my sister that we still have a long way to go and we have to restrict our eating as much as possible, or our food won't last the journey. She agrees, assuring me that she really isn't so hungry after all.

Chapter Two

⪻⪼

We enter a forest.
Treblinka.
Before our eyes—an image of death.
Men to the right—women to the left!

A FTER A SHORT WHILE, THE TRAIN BEGINS TO MOVE. By now it is light outside. We grow uneasy because we see that the train is moving backwards. The train moves slowly and we enter a forest. We look at each other with uncertainty. The answer is: who knows? But soon there appears before our eyes a grim and terrible scene. A scene of . . . death. Through a small opening I see great piles of clothes. I realize that we are lost. Alas, it is hopeless. After a short while the door of the traincar is abruptly thrown open to the accompaniment of fiendish screams—*Raus! Raus!* (Get out! Get out!). I no longer have any doubts about our misfortune. I put my arm around my sister and try to get out of the car as quickly as possible. I leave everything behind. My poor sister asks me why I am leaving our baggage. I reply—It is not necessary . . . I don't manage to say even a few more words to her before we hear a murderous shout—Men to the right, women to the left. I barely have time to kiss her and we are torn apart forever.

Blows begin falling on us from all sides. The murderers drive us in rows into an open space and scream at us to surrender our gold, money and valuables immediately. Anyone who tries to conceal anything will be shot. Nearly all of us part with what we still have. Then we are ordered to undress quickly and tie our shoes together by the laces. Everyone undresses as quickly as possible, because the whips are flying over our heads. Whoever undresses a bit more slowly—is savagely beaten.

Treblinka is built in a professional way. On arrival it might appear to be an ordinary train station. The platform is long and wide enough to accommodate a normal train of as many as forty cars. A few dozen metres from the platform two barracks stand opposite one another. In one, on the right, is stored the food that people bring with them. The barracks on the left is where the women and children undress. The murderers are so considerate that they do not require the women to undress in the open air along with the men. On the way to their deaths, from which there is no return, men and women will meet intimately.

On the left side of the platform stand several wooden structures, among them the kitchen and the workshops. Opposite these are the sleeping quarters. Nearby are the barracks where the SS men live. The SS barracks are provided with every comfort. On the right side of the railway platform there is a big space where clothes, shoes, underwear, bedclothes and other things are gathered. Here several hundred workers work to sort the clothing and carry it to a special place. Every few days the sorted clothing is sent to Germany on lorries.

Opposite the platform where the barracks stand begins the road to the gas chambers, known as the *Schlauch* (pipeline). The road is planted with small trees and looks like a garden path. Down this road, which is covered with a layer of white sand, all must run naked. No-one returns from this road. People driven down this road are beaten mercilessly and stabbed with bayonets, so that after the people have been driven down it, the road is covered in blood.

A special commando, known as the *Schlauch-Kolonne*, cleans the road after every transport. They spread fresh sand so that the next victims will be unaware.

The *Schlauch* road is not long. In a few minutes you find yourself in a white structure, on which a Star of David is painted. On the steps of the structure stands a German, who points to the entrance and smiles—*Bitte, bitte!* The steps lead to a corridor lined with flowers and with long towels hanging on the walls.

The size of the gas chamber is 7 by 7 metres. In the middle of the chamber there are shower-heads through which the gas is introduced. On one of the walls a thick pipe serves as an exhaust to remove the air. Thick felt around the doors of the chamber renders them airtight.

In this building there are some ten gas chambers. At a short distance from the main structure there is a smaller one with three gas chambers. By the doors stand several Germans who shove people inside. Their hands do not rest for a moment as they scream fiendishly—Faster, faster, keep moving!

I am already undressed and look around. I no longer have any doubts about our fate. We are helpless. I notice that in the barracks opposite us, the women and children are undressing, and we can hear their pitiful screams. It is impossible to get near them. We are ordered to line up in rows. We stand as we are ordered to. Those who are still undressing are mercilessly beaten. When nearly all of us are lined up, the guards approach and choose some hundred men from among us, only young ones, and have us stand aside. The others are led away. Where, no one knows. I find myself among the chosen hundred young men. From a distance, I see my friend Rojzman with his son, and, not really knowing whether it is better for him, I gesture to him to run over to me in my group.

We stand for a few minutes until all the other men have been led away and then we are led back to the baggage that the Jews brought with them. Each of us must grab a bundle bigger than himself, and if anyone takes a smaller bundle he is whipped constantly. We are driven to a big space. Along the way guards are posted, arms linked in a human chain, so that no one will escape the whips.

I am astounded by the terrible scene: you see several mountains of piled-up baggage. We are driven to one such stack where parcels of bedclothes and sacks are lying. People stand by the stack sorting the contents. I see that they are all Jews and, running past, try to ask them— Brothers, tell me, what is this? Unfortunately I receive no reply. Each of them tries to turn his head away so as not to have to answer. I ask them again—Tell me, what is going on here? One of them replies—Brother, do not ask. We are lost!

The running back and forth with the bundles happens so fast that I no longer know what is happening to me. We make several round trips, the bundles are cleared away, and we are driven back to the clothes that we took off. We are ordered to retrieve the pairs of shoes which each of us had tied by the laces. We grab the shoes and are driven back to the big open space to a second stack, which is about four storeys high and which consists of nothing but shoes, tens of thousands of pairs of shoes. After the shoes, the clothes that we men had taken off are cleared away. We change direction to another stack, which contains only clothes. After the space is finally cleared, we are driven into the barracks where the women undressed. Before my eyes lie the clothes of the poor women, among them those of my pretty young sister. I look around, but none of the women are there. They have all been led away, driven further on. I am distracted for a moment, pick up a small bundle and try to move on. I am hit so hard with a wire whip that I nearly black out. The murderer screams at me like a stuck pig—You dog, the bundle is too small!

I hardly know what is happening to me. I throw myself to the ground, spread my arms as wide as possible and grab as much as I can. I run out quickly, because the last ones remaining are mercilessly beaten.

We run back and forth several times with the bundles with the whips falling on us every step of the way.

Chapter Three

I am chosen as a barber

I SORT CLOTHING UNTIL THE NEXT TRANSPORTS ARRIVE. Once, when I straighten up, I am beaten till I bleed.

I no longer know where I am in the world. Suddenly, running back for more bundles, I hear one of the murderers, an SS man, shout—Which of you is a barber?

I look around and see that four undressed men already are standing to one side, among them my friend Leybl Goldfarb from our town. I run over to them and announce that I am a barber.

The murderer asks me if I am telling the truth. I answer—*Jawohl!* He tells me to move over to the four others—I am the fifth. Several others try to run over after me, but he does not want to take any more. The answer is—*Es reicht* (That's enough).

He orders us to come with him right away to the storeroom where the sorted-out men's clothes are lying. He orders the Jews working there to give us something to put on, and each of us quickly receives a pair of trousers and a jacket. I ask for a shirt, but the Jew who works there tells me to be quiet and to dress as quickly as possible. He says to me—Brother, you have been saved from death! I quickly put on the trousers and jacket. The other four Jews do the same.

The murderer leads me to another place and orders that we be given shoes. Each of us grabs a pair of shoes and quickly puts them on. We are then led to another place where Jews are sorting parcels and are ordered to stay there and sort. When a new transport arrives, we are to be released, since we are intended for barbering.

I have no notion of barbering and no idea what will happen if I cannot carry out the work. But I tell myself that after all it cannot be worse than dying . . .

As I stand among the piles to be sorted, I notice other men from my transport running past, and suddenly I see my friend Rojzman among them. I yell to him to run over to the German who took me from the previous place and tell him that he, Rojzman, is a barber too. Rojzman runs over to the German and the answer is a whip over his head. Alas, that is the last time I see my friend. He is driven away forever.

We are at once put to work sorting. My friend Leybl stands next to me. We inspect every garment as carefully as possible. On the other side of me stands a worker who has already been here for several days. I want to find out from him what happens here, since, despite the fact that I see the clothes left behind by the victims, I still cannot grasp what is going on. He advises me—Remember, don't talk, try to stay bent over, don't straighten up, or you will feel the whip.

I bend over more deeply and ask him again what happens here.

—Don't you see what is going on here? Here they take the lives of our nearest and dearest. Don't you see that these are the clothes of the poor wretches who come here?

He is afraid to talk too much. The fear here is tremendously strong. I tell him that the five of us were selected from the transport as barbers and I don't know what our work will be. I find out that he too belongs to the barbers, and that our work consists of cutting off the hair of all the women. I want to find out from him how the work is carried out and he answers—You'll see.

I leave him alone and continue to sort the clothes, one by one, just like the others. I look around and see where a lot of suitcases have been placed. Each suitcase contains something different. For example, the main suitcase is for the money that has been found. It quickly fills up with gold, money and valuables. From time to time a special worker, called the *Gold-Jude*, comes around and carries away the filled suitcases. Then there are suitcases for small valuables like watches, others for razors, cigarette lighters and various other things. Everything has to be sorted separately.

My neighbour urges me to select a good, sharp pair of scissors for my work. I find a pair of barber shears and tell my friend Leybl to do the same, since he knows about as much about barbering as I do.

The clock strikes 12:00 and we hear a bugle call. Everyone heads in the direction of the place where we are to be given a midday meal. My friend and I try to stay close to our neighbour, since we don't yet know how things are done here. Everyone tries to get as close to the kitchen as possible. We all stand in rows of five. After a short while we move in the direction of the kitchen. When we come to the kitchen, the window is still closed. We wait several minutes, then, marching in groups of five past the little window, we get the soup. Everyone tries to eat it as fast as possible. Soon we hear the bugle call again. All of us have to stand in rows as before. That has to happen very fast: whoever gets disorientated and doesn't stand in the right place is whipped.

I continue to stay close to my neighbour. With a few minutes to spare, I try to learn from him how to go about the work. His explanation is as follows: when a fresh transport arrives, the same murderer rushes over. His name is Kiewe; he has been here a long time. He yells out— Barbers! and we have to report at once. We are led to the gas chamber where our brothers and sisters are gassed. My neighbour points out that we have to cut the hair as quickly as possible. It must all happen extraordinarily fast. The murderers are standing around and whoever cuts slowly is badly beaten.

The bugle call sounds again and we get ready. Each group is inspected and then we move, each to his place. The work continues. I try to go through the clothing as quickly as possible, but I forget that it is forbidden to stand upright. I straighten up for a few minutes and suddenly one of the bandits approaches and starts to whip me without stopping. Then he asks me if I know why I was whipped. I answer—*Jawohl!* The bandit has cut me in the head and blood runs over my face. I find a bottle of water and put a wet rag to my head. My neighbour yells—Remember to stay bent over, or you'll get more lashes!

I bend over. With one hand I hold the wet rag to my head, and with the other I sort the clothes. It is a long time before I stop bleeding. My face is bloody, and my friend quietly tells me to wash it, because anyone with the marks of blows on his face is shot.

I try to wash myself and return to work. After a while, my foreman orders me to take the sorted bundles to the warehouse. He shows me the way to the warehouse and warns me to make it fast, especially on the way back, when I am not carrying anything. I grab a parcel and head in the direction of the storage area for men's coats. I put down my load and see that every few metres there is a great pile of various kinds of clothing and every pile has a sign indicating what is in it.

I hurry back to my work, and by carrying the bundles I become familiar with the place and know where everything is located. The work goes much too quickly. Every few minutes the murderers come with whips in their hands and shout—Faster. Get moving!

From time to time they order the workers to lie down and give them a few hard lashes. After the blows you have to get up quickly and run back to work. That is what our work is like.

Chapter Four

❧

First night in the barracks.

*Moyshe Ettinger tells how he saved himself
and cannot forgive himself.*

*The evening prayer is recited and
Kaddish is said for the dead.*

I T IS 6:00 IN THE EVENING. WE HEAR A BUGLE CALL. We stop work and stand to attention in groups of five. The foreman, a Jewish engineer called Galewski, counts us and makes his report. We hear an orchestra playing. We turn right and go in the direction of the kitchen. The kitchen window is opened and we approach it in rows to get our soup. We head for the barracks, which stand opposite the kitchen. The barracks are filled to capacity and we have to lie on the ground.

I look at my friend Leybl and he at me, and our tears pour like rain. Each of us asks the other why he is crying. I cannot answer. I have lost the power of speech. We try to comfort and calm one another as much as possible. Leybl, I say to him, yesterday at this time my young sister was still alive. He answers—And my whole family, my brothers and twelve thousand poor Jews from my town.

And yet we are alive and witness this great misfortune and are so hardened that we can eat and endure the heartbreak. How can one be so strong, have such unnatural strength to endure? As we stand there, we notice a friend, Moyshe Ettinger, from our town. He falls on us sobbing. After he has calmed down a bit, he tells us that yesterday he was running naked to the gas chamber. Along the way he happened upon a mound of clothing and crawled into the middle of it. He grabbed a pair of trousers and a jacket from the pile and put them on. Not far away he saw a Jew marching past. He begged him to save him and find him a pair of shoes. Fortunately, the worker found a pair and brought them to him. Then he worked his way out of his hiding place and stood near the pile of clothing and began sorting it. The workers standing next to him helped him and told him what to do. In that way he saved himself from death.

Now he stands next to us and weeps. He cannot forgive himself for having saved himself when his wife and child went to their deaths. We are all as if drugged. Yesterday my family and I were living and now—all are dead. Each of us stands as if turned to stone. I weep for my fate, for what I have lived to see.

At that moment I hear how to the left of the barracks the miserable survivors stand to say the evening prayers, and after praying they recite Kaddish for the dead with tears in their eyes. Kaddish wakes me up. I look closely: yes, all who are here are wretched orphans and accursed individuals. I become almost wild and shout at them—To whom are you reciting Kaddish? You still believe? In what do you believe, whom are you thanking? Are you thanking the Lord for his mercy in taking away our brothers and sisters, our fathers and mothers? No, no! It is not true; there is no God. If there were a God, he would not allow such misfortune, such transgression, where innocent small children, only just born, are killed, where people who want only to do honest work and make themselves useful to the world are killed! And you, living witnesses of the great misfortune, remain thankful. Whom are you thanking?

My grief-stricken friend Leybl tries to calm me—Calm yourself. You are right. Yesterday all my brothers and sisters with their little ones were alive, and today they are no longer in this world.

He is trying to calm me, and he is beside himself and begs me—Yekhiel, don't shout, you know where we are . . .

He himself is shouting louder than I am.

We fall to the ground from fatigue and cannot get up. I lie there and remind myself that I wronged my poor sister. A few minutes before her death I dissuaded her from eating a piece of bread and she was driven hungry to her death. Did she forgive me? The murderers robbed all of us of our understanding.

We lie like that in our pain. The clock strikes 9:00 in the evening. The barracks are locked, the lights turned off. I lie on the ground all night.

Chapter Five

❧

I work as a barber.

My sister's dress.
The last wish of an old Jewish woman.

The laughter of an eighteen-year-old girl . . .

We sing a song.

AT 5:00 IN THE MORNING WE ARE AWAKENED BY the alarm and we tear ourselves from our sleep. We walk to the kitchen. Each of us receives coffee and bread, and at 6:00—off to work. I discover that there are several groups of sorters. Each group takes its place separately, and after all of them are counted, some seven hundred people in total, each group is led away to work with its *Kapo* and foreman at the head. I am given the same work as the day before, sorting clothes. While sorting I find the dress that my sister was wearing. I stop, grasp the dress, hold it for a moment and examine it from every angle. I show it to my neighbour. He forgets himself for a moment and pities me. Then immediately he shouts—You are forgetting yourself. Naturally, who can help himself?

Our fate is so wretched. But remember, you can get the whip for that.

I tear off a piece of the dress and hide it in my pocket. (I had that piece of the dress with me for ten months, the whole time I was in Treblinka.)

The clock strikes 8:00. The foreman suddenly calls out—Barbers!

All the barbers, ten men, five old and five new ones, stand next to him. He asks if each of us has shears (we have all provided ourselves with them) and then leads us away to the evil gas chambers, where the living are transformed into the dead.

He leads us into the first cell, which is open to the corridor and to the outside. It is a fine summer's day. The sun's rays reach us. Long benches are set out and next to them dozens of suitcases.

The murderer orders us to take our places. Each of us stands behind a suitcase. A band of Ukrainians surrounds us, with whips in their hands and rifles on their shoulders. The *Kommandant* of Treblinka comes in—a tall, stout murderer of about fifty. He orders us to work fast. After five cuts the hair must be all cut off. We have to make sure that no hair falls on the ground, and the suitcases must be fully packed. He ends his order this way—If not, you will be whipped, you accursed dogs!

We stand as if paralyzed. A few minutes pass and we hear pitiful screams. Naked women appear. In the corridor stands a murderer who tells them to run into the room where we are. They are beaten murderously and driven with cries of "Faster, faster!"

I stare wide-eyed at the victims and cannot believe my eyes. Every woman sits down next to a barber. Next to me a young woman sits down. My hands are paralyzed and I cannot move my fingers. The women sit opposite us and wait for us to cut off their beautiful hair, and their weeping is pitiful and terrible.

My friend next to me shouts—Remember, you will be lost, because a murderer is standing there and can see you working slowly!

I force open the fingers of my dirty hand, cut off the woman's hair and throw it into the suitcase like every one else. The woman stands up. I see that she is dazed from the blows she has received. She asks me where to go and I show her the second entryway, on the left. Before I have time to turn around, a second woman is already sitting down. She takes my hand and wants to kiss me—I beg you, tell me, what do they do with us? Is this already the end?

She weeps and begs me to tell her if it is a difficult death, if it takes long, if people are gassed or electrocuted . . .

I do not reply. She will not leave me alone and begs me to tell her, because she knows that in any case she is lost. Nevertheless I cannot tell the truth and calm her. The whole conversation lasts a few seconds, as long as it takes me to cut her hair. I turn my head away, because I cannot look her in the eye. The murderer standing near us shouts—*Los! Schneller die Haare schneiden!* (Come on! Cut the hair faster!) The woman is bewildered. After a bit she jumps up and runs out.

One victim after the other sits down and the shears cut and cut the hair without stopping. Weeping and screaming can be heard. Many women tear off pieces of their own living flesh and we have to look on and are forbidden to say anything.

An elderly woman sits down in front of me. I cut her hair and she begs me to grant her a last wish before her death: to cut her hair a bit more slowly, because after her, next to my friend, stands her young daughter, and she wants them to go to their deaths together. I try to oblige the woman and at the same time I ask my friend to speed up his cutting. I want to fulfill the last request of the elderly woman. But unfortunately the murderer screams at me and whips my head. I have to hurry and cannot help the woman any more. She has to run without her daughter . . .

Continuing to cut hair, I suddenly hear a shout. I turn and see a young girl of about eighteen run inside and begin shouting at all the women—What is the matter with you? You ought to be ashamed! For whom are you crying? You should be laughing! Let our enemies see that we are not going to our deaths as cowards. The murderers enjoy our weeping!

All stand as if frozen to the spot. The murderers look around. They become even wilder and the girl laughs in their faces until she leaves.

From among the wretched victims a young, pretty girl sits down in front of me. She begs me—Do not cut off all my hair. What will I look like?

I cannot reply. What can I say to her? I try to calm her . . .

A woman sits down before me. She tears out her hair-pins and shouts at me—Faster! Do what you want. You can even cut some of the flesh out of my scalp. I know that I am lost . . .

Yes, we are all lost.

An older woman begs me to tell her if all the men are kept as labourers. She knows that she is going to her death. Still, she will be happy if her son, who came with her, remains alive. I calm her with my answer and she thanks me. She is content that her son will remain alive and take revenge on the murderers . . .

Thus hundreds of women pass through with weeping and shouting and I have become an automaton that cuts off their hair.

Suddenly the shoving of the next group of victims is interrupted because the gas chambers are over-full. The murderer standing by the door of the cell announces that there will be a break of half an hour and goes away. Some Ukrainians and several SS men remain with us. I look around and think: Good God, what kind of hell is this? The murderers force us to cut off the hair of our sisters a few minutes before their deaths and we, the temporarily spared, do it in the shadow of the whips. We have been deprived of our reason and are the tools of criminals. My friend who worked with me sorting clothes asks me quietly—Why have you changed so much? I don't recognize you!

I don't reply and he leaves me alone.

It doesn't take long, and several murderers come in and order us to sing a song. But only a beautiful song.

The old barbers already know what that means: if we don't sing, we will be mercilessly beaten, and out of fear several begin to sing. I am as if paralyzed: over there in the cell they gas people and we are supposed to sing! A murderer, noticing that my mouth is closed, screams at me—You dog, do you want to get it on your mug?

I open my mouth as if I were singing. Alas, we have to sing and amuse the murderers.

From time to time one of them goes out into the corridor and looks through a small window to ascertain if the victims are dead.

Half an hour passes in this way. A murderer comes in and announces that work is resuming. We must once again take our places in order to receive new victims. Once again we hear pitiful cries and soon naked women appear.

The work proceeds without hindrance. The whole transport is disposed of in an hour: several thousand people have been gassed.

Chapter Six

❦

New transports.
To the gas chambers with "Shema Yisrael."
Our first decision to escape.
My last days in Camp I.

THE WORK IS FINISHED. OUR SECTION CHIEF COMES in and announces that the transport has been liquidated. We close the suitcases and place them on the side. We are immediately escorted to the open space and in the shadow of the dreaded whips we must forget that we have cut the hair of thousands of women. Now once again we have to search for money, gold and valuables for the murderers and again sort clothes. The Chief notifies our foreman, Scher from Czestochowa, that by 12:00 the pile of *Scheisse* (shit) must be cleared away. From time to time SS men come to the square and order us to pick out good-quality suits and good watches for them and fine dresses for their wives. We must hurry for the pile must at all costs be cleared away by noon.

The clock strikes 12:00. We are already standing by the kitchen when we hear the locomotive entering the camp again, dragging fresh victims with it. The same freight cars appear and we hear the doors thrown open quickly, and as always everyone is driven out of the cars with blows from rifle butts and whips. A few minutes later the head murderer of the camp appears and shouts—Barbers, step out! We have not yet eaten our midday soup but are at once led back to the gas chambers, to more of our filthy work. And the same terrifying picture: more wretched souls appear, from the town of Ostrowice. In a bit over an hour it is all over for them.

Before me sits a young woman. I cut her hair and she grabs my hand and begs me to remember that I too am a Jew. She knows that she is lost. But remember, she says, you see what is being done to us. That's why my wish for you is that you will survive and take revenge for our innocent blood, which will never rest . . .

I reply quietly—My dear woman, the same fate awaits me. I am a Jew, after all.

The woman has not had time to get up when a murderer who is walking between the benches lashes her head with his whip. Blood shows on her shorn head. She jumps up and runs where all are running.

We finish our work and remain standing at our places for a while, because the way out is occupied by the naked men being driven to the gas chambers. They run through a chain of murderers who stand on both sides and beat them. The Jews run with their hands raised, fingers spread wide, chanting continuously—*Sh'ma Yisrael, Sh'ma Yisrael* (Hear,

O Israel). With these words on their lips they are driven to their deaths.

The stream of victims comes to an end, the iron door is hermetically shut, and the last cries of the victims are silenced. The murderers appear and we are led back to the square, because the noon break is over. We sort clothes at a rapid pace in order the make room for new bundles. I sort then carry the bundles in various directions.

The afternoon passes in that way. The clock strikes 6:00. Hearing the signal, we stop working and take our places for roll-call. After counting us, the Jewish head *Kapo*, Galewski, announces the number of prisoners to the chief killer, Kiewe. He then orders—*Rechts um!* (Right face!) in the direction of the kitchen.

As we did yesterday, each of us receives his soup and heads for the barracks. I stand with my friend Leybl and with Moyshe Ettinger and the tears pour from us without stopping. We finally begin to understand the whole catastrophe that takes place here, that this is a factory that swallows victims without stopping: yesterday twelve thousand, today fifteen thousand, and so on without end . . . We want to find out what is done with the victims after they are dead, but we are unable to, because there, where the corpses are, is Camp 2, which is entirely isolated from us, and we have no contact with the Jews who work there.

We ponder and ponder and ask ourselves: what now? And we decide that at all costs we must look for possibilities of escape, because at some point without warning we are in any case going to be killed.

We decide that, starting tomorrow, each of us will begin to collect as much money as he can from what we find while working, trying in the next few days to collect tens of thousands of zlotys, and at the same time we will try to find a way to escape.

Meanwhile the clock strikes 9:00. The lights are turned off. Exhausted and depressed, we throw ourselves to the ground. We groan for a time with the heavy pain in our hearts, then fall asleep.

We sleep through the night and at 4:30 we hear the signal. We awake from our deep sleep. I ask around to see if I can obtain a little water to wash myself with. My friend tells me that he hasn't washed in the ten days since he came here. We march out to our breakfast of coffee and bread. I am able to save a little water to wash with. We march to the roll-call, and, after being counted, we are led by our *Kapo* and foreman to the square for work.

My friend Leybl and I get to work. When we find larger bills we try to hide them so that no murderer will notice, otherwise we will get a bullet in the head. We collect the money carefully and hide it in the coat I am wearing. I work that way for a couple of hours and gather several thousand zlotys. By noon I have about 5,000 zlotys. My friend Leybl has somewhat more. At the noon break we decide to collect as much money as we can, since without money we are lost even if we succeed in escaping.

In the afternoon the work goes quickly. I once again find several thousand zlotys. It is about 2:00 in the afternoon. While sorting I hear, not far from me, a murderer call— *Komm' her!* (Come here!) I drop what I am doing and run

Chil Rajchman was the first born of the six children of Java and Abraham Froim. His mother (lower left) died of an illness a few years before the war began. Chil persuaded his brother, Moñek, to escape to the part of eastern Poland occupied by the Soviets; he survived, but most of the family members died, or were assumed to have died, during the war. His sister Ratza (upper left) married, had a child, and was later murdered in the Lodz ghetto. Chil and another sister Rivke were deported to Treblinka where she died. He was never certain what became of his younger sister Ruska (lower right), his little brother Isaac, or his father (upper right). These photographs, miraculously saved, are the only record of the prewar years.

In the fall of 1941, Himmler created three death camps. Belzec was opened in March of 1942; Sobibor in May, and Treblinka in June. More than 330,000 Jews from the Warsaw ghetto were deported to Treblinka (left and below).

Above, Hitler and Himmler (center) inspect Treblinka. In the spring of 1943 Himmler established the practice of cremation to dispose of the bodies of those killed at the camp.

Treblinka was governed by Franz Stangl (opposite) from August 1942 to August 1943. He created ten new gas chambers and reorganized the camp to further "industrialize" the process of killing and disposal.

Treblinka I

1. Entrance
2. Guard Post
3. SS Living quarters
4. Armory
5. Gas pump
6. Garage
7. Administration and Commandant's living quarters
8. Service building
9. Prisoners' barracks
10. Bakery
11. Grocery store
12. "Goldjuden" or goldworks workshop
13. Ukranian guards' living quarters
14. Zoo
15. Stables
16. Prisoners' barracks
17. Prisoners' kitchen
18. Locksmith and ironworks
19. Toilets
20. Assembly area
21. Train arrival platform
22. Property storehouse made to look like a train station
23. Receiving and sorting area
24. Women's undressing room
25. Hairdresser
26. Suitcase depot
27. Selection area
28. "Lazarett" (execution site)
29. "Der Schlauch" (access to gas chambers)

Treblinka II

30. Gas chambers (phase 2)
31. Gas chambers (phase 1)
32. Burial pits
33. Pyres for burning dead bodies
34. Prisoners' barracks

Key

═══	Main road
≡ ≡ ≡ ≡	Secondary road
┿┿┿┿┿	Railroad
▬▬▬	Barbed wire
⌇⌇	Dirt wall
⊠	Watch tower
⊙	Well
🌲	Woods

Camp # 2, which contained the extermination area, was relatively small, 600 meters by 400 meters, and surrounded by barbed wire. A fake train station was built in December 1942 at the arrival platform to conceal from the passengers the nature of this final destination. The camp received up to six trainloads a day and was operating at maximum capacity.

Map of Treblinka

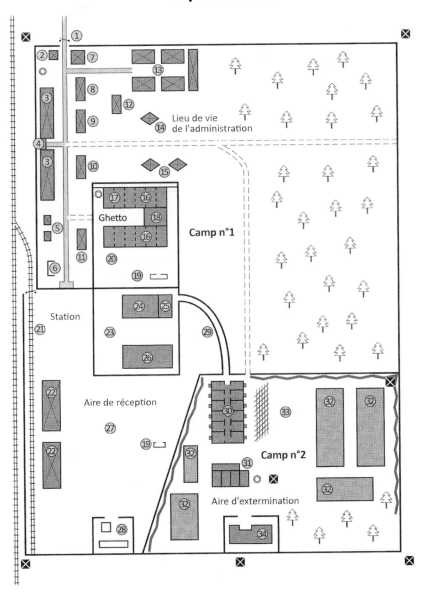

Source : Yitzhak Arad, Belzec, Sobibor, Treblinka.
The Operation Reinhardt Death Camps, Indiana University Press, 1987. © Donatien Cassan

The SS of Treblinka and Sobibor celebrate.

The pace of arrival of the rail convoys decreased in January 1932, dropping more rapidly after June. Franz Stangl continued update the camp and in the Spring of 1943 he created a zoo for the Ukranian guards and the SS.

Kurt Franz joined the SS before the war and worked in euthanasia centers. He was sent to Treblinka in the fall of 1942, becoming Stengl's right hand man. Six months later he succeeded Stengl. He was arrested in Germany in 1959 and sentenced to life in prison. The photographs he took at Treblinka (lower left and following spread) were seized at the time of his arrest.

The dog Bari, the size of a young cow, often accompanied his master Kurt Franz on his rounds of the camp. Franz would set him on a prisoner yelling, "Man, bite him".

At the camp's darkest hour, twelve to
fifteen thousand people were gassed in
a single day. The primary preoccupa-
tion of the executioners was to find an
efficient way to bury the bodies. To this
end they dug pits 50 meters long by 25
wide and 10 meters deep. By the end of
1942 the new bodies are no longer buried
but burned on huge pyres; the filled pits
were opened and those bodies exhumed
to be burned. The operation fell under
the name of Action 1005, named after the
officer in charge. The order stated that
all traces of mass extermination must be
hidden. Photographs of the prisoners and
the mass graves were strictly forbidden.

A small clandestine movement arose among the prisoners of camp # 1 at the beginning of 1943. The prime movers were Zhelo Bloch (opposite) Rudolf Masarek, Yankel Wiernik (across). The engineer Galewski (below) was the leader of the group. Their plan for an uprising involved breaking into the armory, capturing the guards, destroying camp buildings, and escaping into the neighboring forests.

Smoke rising from Treblinka during the uprising.

The uprising began on Monday August 2, 1943. The prisoners set the camp's wooden structures on fire but the gas chambers, built of brick, were not destroyed. At the time there were 850 prisoners in the camp of whom 350 were killed by guards and within a few hours an additional 250 prisoners were captured in the surrounding area and executed. Those prisoners who remained were transferred in October 1943 to Sobibor where they were killed by gassing. As few as 60 people survived, including Chil Rajchman.

The only known photo of an active burial pit in Treblinka in 1943.

Above, a photograph of a burial pit in Treblinka taken after the war.
The number of victims of Treblinka is difficult to determine because of the
systemic destruction of the bodies, the secrecy required by the Nazis, and the
missing and incomplete archives. At the Düsseldorf Court of Assize Helmut
Kraunsnick, Director of the Institute of Contemporary History of Munich
gave an estimate of a minimum of 700,000 Jews. Another expert, called in for
a second trial in 1970, raised the estimate to 900,000.

Chil Rajchman (left) and his brother Moñek are the only surviving family members. When they met after the war, Chil did not tell his brother about his life as a prisoner at Treblinka, waiting a while before giving him his notes about his time there.

Ten former SS officers from Treblinka are judged by the Düsseldorf Court of Assize from October 1964 to October 1965. Kurt Franz, Arthur Matthes, Willy Mentz and August Miete are sentenced to life in prison but Albert Rum, Erwin Lambert, Franz Süchomel, Otto Stadie and Gustav Müntzberger receive sentences of only three to twelve years. One officer, Otto Horn, is acquitted.

Franz Stengl (opposite) is arrested in Brazil, extradited to Germany, and appears before the court in 1970; he receives a life sentence.

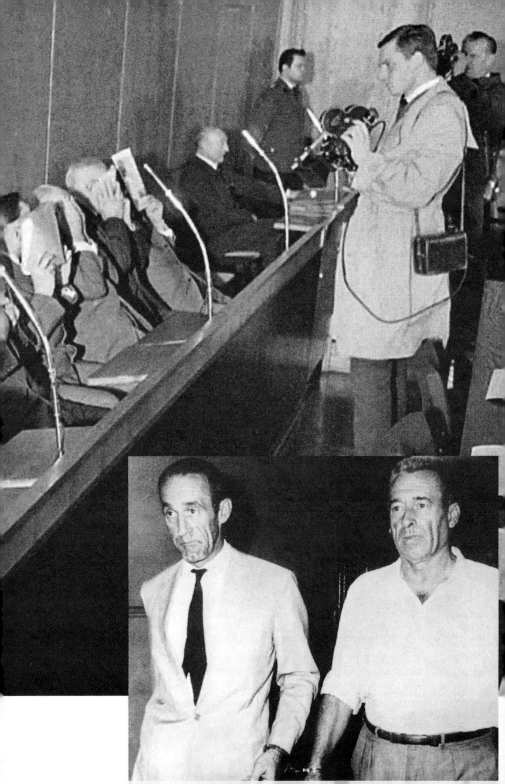

Chil Rajchman with his three sons José, Andrés, and Daniel, in 1986.

Between 1958 and 1963 the Polish Government create a series of monuments to the memory of the victims on grounds of Treblinka. One monument memorializes the pediatrician Janusz Korczak.

over to him. He tells me to remain standing there. There are soon about twenty of us standing there and we do not know what will happen to us. I see that more and more workers are being sent over. Fearing that we may be searched, I take off the coat in which the money is hidden. I throw it to the side with the excuse that I'm hot. After a few minutes I and about thirty others are led to the courtyard, where we all undress and are carefully searched to see if any of us has hidden money or valuables. The murderers find one man with money. He is brutally beaten, taken aside and shot.

As I am one of the last to be inspected, I am able to search my pockets and find a 100-zloty banknote. I do not become flustered and put the banknote quickly into my mouth. The murderers do not notice. They take away our pocket knives and razor blades. They line us up in groups of five and lead us towards where the victims are driven to the gas chambers. But instead of the gas chambers, we are led to the second camp, which is far worse than the gas chambers.

Chapter Seven

❦

Treblinka—Camp 2.
I become a carrier of corpses.
Gold teeth are extracted from the dead.
The technique of carrying corpses.

N O SOONER DO WE CROSS THE THRESHOLD OF THE wretched camp than we are greeted with a hail of lashes from the whips, which fall unceasingly upon us. We are immediately driven to a job that consists of taking sand in barrows from one pile and carrying it to another pile. In the first minutes I think I am going to pass out. I don't know what I am carrying and where I am carrying it. Nevertheless, after running several times to the pile where we pour out the sand, I see that we are pouring it onto corpses that have been thrown into a pit. I am unable to gather my thoughts because they do not leave us a second to rest. We load the sand with the greatest possible speed, grab the barrow immediately and run, dump the sand onto the victims and then run back again. The sweat is pouring from our faces. I throw off my jacket, but that doesn't help. At every step there stand the murderers who lash every one of us on the head with their long whips. I expend my last ounce of strength and am no longer able to stand. A murderer approaches me and beats me without cease—You dog, my whip is broken by this time every day, but today it's still in one piece!

He beats me without stopping. I am foaming at the mouth and feel that my strength is at an end. The same is true of my friends. In the distance stands a murderer observing our work. He calls over one after another of us, tells each one to undress and descend into the pit. The victims have to bend over and receive a bullet in the head. They then fall on top of the corpses that lie spread out below.

After about fifteen minutes perhaps twenty of my comrades are missing. Our group is thinning out. I look around and see that there is almost no-one left. I am sure that my turn will come in a few minutes. I don't know where I get the extraordinary strength to throw myself into my work, to the point where the murderer standing next to me and beating me says to me—You work well. I won't shoot you.

I am unsteady on my feet and can't go on . . . The comrade working next to me begs me to keep going. He is a little stronger than I am and tries to make things easier for me. He fills my barrow with sand so I can have a minute to rest.

It is about 4:00 in the afternoon. Of the thirty fellow-inmates who came here, I see that no more than six remain. One after the other had to undress, go down into the pit and receive a bullet in his head. We did not hear so much as a groan. Down in the pit stand two workers who lay out the dead.

Suddenly a new murderer appears. He tells us to put down our barrows and leads us to a different job. He tells us to take hold of what look like ladder-shaped litters. The litters are bloody. Two of us grab a litter and are driven to a distant building. In it are scattered piles of stiff bodies to a height of one storey. These are the people who were gassed.

We have no time to think because the whips fly over our heads. I don't know what to do. I look on for a while, then see how Jews come running with empty litters, put them down quickly and run over to the pile of corpses. One of them takes the dead body by one hand, a second by the other hand. They pull it off the pile, drag it onto the litter and run off as quickly as possible.

I try to do the same, but it is hard for me; I am stunned by the picture before my eyes. I grab the hand of a corpse that has several other corpses lying on top of it. My comrade grabs the corpse's other hand and we try to pull it down. But we cannot. One of the murderers sees that we have been standing there for several minutes and runs over and beats us without stopping. The blood is pouring down our faces. But we pay no attention to that and try to pull out another corpse. We succeed. Seeing how things are done, we drag the corpse quickly onto the bloody litter and run in the direction where everyone is running. Along the way we are once again accompanied by the whips of the murderers who stand on both sides. Being new, we don't orientate ourselves right away and are beaten even more.

Along the way stand the "dentists" who inspect every corpse to see if it has any gold teeth. Not knowing about this, I don't stop, because I'm afraid of being beaten. A dentist sees that the corpse I am carrying has gold teeth. He stops me and won't let me go any further since he has to extract the teeth. He shouts to me to stand still and blocks my path. I shout to him—Why won't you let me run? I'll get whipped on account of you. He reassures me that by standing next to him I won't be beaten. He tells me quietly that if he lets a corpse with false teeth pass him by he will get a bullet to the head. I see how his hands are trembling. After a few seconds he tells me—On your way!

I break into a line of carriers who are running with corpses one after another. We come to a deep pit and I try to imitate what the carriers running ahead of me are doing. I try, like them, to dump the corpse by tilting the litter to one side. But the head of the corpse gets stuck between the rungs of the litter and we can't do anything about it. We try to pull out the head of the corpse, but we are unable to. Meanwhile we are delaying those who are waiting behind us. The worker, a Jew, who lays the bodies out straight like herrings shouts to me to lay the litter down on the ground quickly and pull the head of the corpse out from between the rungs. A murderer standing near the pit runs over and rains down blows on us with his whip until we finally succeed in pulling out the head of the corpse and then run off with the empty litter in the direction of the heap of dead bodies.

During the time I am delayed by pulling out the head of the dead man the chain of workers is broken, and as the first to arrive I receive supplemental beatings. By now every part of my body is in pain and I am at a loss what to do.

We arrive at the grim mound. I quickly throw the litter down and I run over and pull down a corpse from the top layer. Though I see a bandit coming, intending to beat us, I pay no attention and throw the corpse face down onto the litter. The bandit detains and beats me.

A carrier running past shouts to me to put the litter down and turn the corpse right side up and make sure that the head is resting on a board, because if it lies between the rungs it will be stuck when the body is dumped. I put down the litter, turn the victim over, and we run off.

Running back and forth several times I finally see what things look like in the deep pit: several laborers stand in the pit, all of them Jews, and lay out the dead bodies one next to the other. That is how the work proceeds. The pit becomes more and more full. There can be no question of resting for a while because we have to run one after the other, without a break. We run back and forth. The two hours that pass in this way, until evening, seem to me like a year.

The clock strikes 6:00. We run one after the other with our litters to the shed where the litters and shovels are stored. All must be put away correctly, otherwise we get the whip.

Finally we assemble for roll-call. After being counted, to the accompaniment of music, we are driven into a barracks surrounded by barbed wire.

Chapter Eight

❧

*My comrade Yankl chooses me for his partner
to carry corpses.*

A sweet dream about my dead mother.

The avenue of hanged Jews.

The columns march out to work.

My comrade's bloody drink.

The jump into the well.

I FALL OVER AND CANNOT MOVE. I LIE THERE FOR A while and hear a shout from the kitchen, ordering us to go and get our coffee. I can barely stand. We are driven from the barracks and once again line up in groups of five to proceed to the kitchen. It takes a couple of minutes before the little window is opened. One after the other we receive a piece of bread and a little muddy water which is called coffee. I have a burning thirst and drink all the coffee without eating the bread, despite the fact that I am starving. The eating ends and we go back to the barracks. I am like a dead man myself. I look around and see that each of us is bruised and bloody.

Groans are heard from all sides. Everyone weeps over his wretched fate. I lie in pain and weep for what I have lived to see. Next to me lies another man who groans just as much as I do. I try to find out something about him. He tells me he is from Czestochowa and that his name is Yankl. We become friendly and he tells me a secret, which is that he has been here for ten days. He points out that no one knows this because none of us know each other. It is very rare for a labourer to last as long as he has. Every day tens of labourers are shot and new labourers are taken from the most recent transports. That way none of us get to know each other. He tells me that two days ago more than a hundred labourers were shot. He informs me that whoever has a bruise on his face is doomed. For that reason he advises me to pay attention and avoid receiving blows to the face insofar as possible. I tell him how many blows I have received and he laughs: here that is nothing new and he is used to it. But at every word he groans—*Oy*, everything hurts . . .

I ask him if we can carry a litter together. He doesn't want to, because he will get additional beatings as a result of my inexperience. I beg him and promise that I will adapt myself to his routine and do everything he tells me to do. He finally agrees and advises me that at roll-call the next morning I should stand next to him, because running to work is a veritable madhouse and whoever is left without a partner gets whipped.

We continue to talk for a while, and my friend Yankl falls asleep on the hard boards. I lie there and feel every part of me aching. I don't know how I will be able to get up in the morning. I lie there and think: where am I actually? In hell. A hell with demons. We wait for death, which can come at any moment, in a few days at best. And for the price of a few days of life we have to dirty our hands and help the bandits do their work. No, we must not do it!

I fall asleep and dream of my honest, faithful mother, who died fifteen years ago. I was fifteen years old at the time. My mother weeps along with me over our fate. She died young. She was thirty-eight when she was torn from us and left us behind. To await such a death? Would it not have been better if the rest of us had not survived? How good it is that my mother did not live to be tortured, to experience a ghetto, poverty, hunger and at the end, Treblinka: to have her hair torn away, to be gassed, then tossed into a pit like tens of thousands of other dead people. I am happy that she did not live to experience that.

My headache wakes me up. Everything hurts and I cannot lie still. I try to turn over and unintentionally bump into my friend Leybl. He wakes up and cries—Murderer, what do you want from me? I try to apologize, but he answers with a groan—*Oy, oy* . . . I try not to touch him again. I want to fall asleep, but I cannot. The night passes slowly like a year, until finally we hear the shout—*Aufstehen*! (Get up!) People tear themselves out of their sleep, and everyone tries to stand near the door, which is still closed.

I notice that opposite me is dangling a man who has hanged himself. I point this out to my neighbor, but he waves dismissively and shows me that further along there are two more people hanging—That is nothing new here. Actually today there are fewer hanging than usual. He tells me that every day several bodies of hanged men are thrown out and nobody pays attention to such details.

I look at the hanging bodies and envy them for being at rest. After a short while the door is thrown open and we are driven out to the kitchen. We get coffee and I still have the piece of bread from yesterday. Most of the Jews just drink the black coffee. The clock strikes 5:30 and we hear a shout—*Antreten!* (Fall in!) We all run out. I see how each of us tries to stand next to another one to make a pair and I try to stand next to my comrade. Fortunately we find each other and are able to stand together.

As usual we are counted quickly. The gate is opened and we are let out: first, a group that works in the machine shop. Those are the mechanics who work on the automobile engine from which the gas is piped to the gas chambers. They rush off to work because a transport has arrived and the preparations to receive it must get under way.

Then the "dentist" group is let out. They run quickly into their cell. They have to grab their dental pliers as fast as possible and run to the open space in order to inspect the bodies and extract the false teeth of the dead.

After the "dentists" the carpenters are let out. Their work consists of building barracks and interior structures.

After them comes the *Schlauch* (tube) group. Their job consists of removing the blood of the victims spilled on the way to the gas chambers. Everything is covered with sand so no trace will remain. After cleaning the road they enter the gas chambers and wash the walls and floors. There must be no trace of blood. The entrances to the gas chambers are opened and a painter gives the walls a fresh coat of paint. Everything must be spotless before receiving new contingents in the cells.

After the *Schlauch* workers comes the *Rampe* (ramp) group. Those are the Jews who work at the gas chambers when a transport has already been gassed. At a signal, the exterior doors are opened and it is time for the *Rampe* workers to remove the corpses. This work is extraordinarily difficult, as the dead are tightly pressed one against the other.

After the *Rampe* workers, the group of kitchen workers comes out. The remaining inmates are then counted. Some of them are assigned to carry corpses and the rest are sent to the sand piles. I notice that the workers who have been here for several days try to avoid the work of carrying sand, because the *Scharführer* (platoon leader) of the sand workers, nicknamed "The White Man," is a specialist in shooting. At roll call he often shows up by himself because he has shot his workers down to the last man.

My friend and I work as carriers. The day, as usual, is extraordinarily difficult. We get so many lashes that our feet can no longer carry us. A sip of water is not to be had. Our lips burn with thirst. It is no use begging or crying. All you get are blows, blows without end.

My comrade with whom I'm carrying a litter notices, while standing for a moment near one of the "dentists," that the bowl into which the "dentist" throws the bloody teeth contains a little water. He throws himself on the ground and drinks the water together with the blood. He gets whipped, but he drinks.

The day is especially difficult. There is a transport today of eighteen thousand people, and all the gas chambers are active.

We work. From time to time it happens that carriers throw down their litters and jump into the deep well that stands near the death chambers and in that way end their accursed lives.

Finally the clock strikes 6:00. There is a shout—*Antreten!*—and we fall in. Our *Scharführer* (Section Chief), Mathias, orders us to sing a pretty song. We have to sing. It is almost an hour before we return to the barracks.

Chapter Nine

I join the "dentist" commando.

Forty hours in the gas chambers.

The mad rush before and after the gassing of the victims.

The technique of "dental" work.

I am whipped for letting through a corpse with false teeth.

AFTER FOUR WEEKS OF WORKING AS A CARRIER, I succeeded in getting into the "dentists" commando. There were nineteen dentists and I was the twentieth.

When *Scharführer* Mathias returned from leave, he ascertained at roll-call that there were nineteen men in the group of dentists. He ordered the *Kapo* of the dentists, Dr. Zimmermann, an acquaintance of mine, to raise the number of dentists to twenty. That was around 3 November [1942]. At that time the transports were increasing once again and more dentists were needed. When Dr. Zimmermann announced that he is looking for a "dentist", I stepped out and declared that I was a dentist. Other people also declared themselves as dentists, but Dr. Zimmermann chose me and got me into his group.

We marched off to our work.

In the building containing the three smaller gas chambers there was an additional wooden shed, which was entered via the corridor that led to the gas chambers. In the shed stood a long table at which the "dentists" worked. In a corner of the shed stood a locked trunk in which were kept the gold and platinum crowns from the teeth of the corpses, as well as the diamonds that were sometimes found in the crowns, along with the money and jewels that were found under the bandages on the naked bodies or in the women's vaginas. Once a week the trunk was emptied by Mathias or Karl Spetzinger, his adjutant. Next to the table stood long benches on which we used to sit tightly crowded together and do our work. On the table were placed dishes with extracted teeth as well as various dental tools.

Our work consisted of scraping out and cleaning the metal from the plaster of the fillings and from the natural teeth. An additional task was to separate the crowns from the bridges and then clean and sort them. For that purpose there was a special blowtorch which melted the rubber. The "dentists" were divided into specialized groups. Five men worked with the white false teeth, others with metal teeth, and two specialists were occupied with sorting the metals, especially white gold, yellow gold, platinum and ordinary metal. The "dentists" used to sit at their work under the direction of Dr. Zimmermann, who was a very decent human being. Germans used to come to him when they had some special business.

Before going on leave they used to come to us to pick out a couple of beautiful stones for themselves, or some foreign currency.

In the shed stood a small stove. On one wall of the shed there were two small windows, which looked out onto the open space in front of the building with the ten big gas chambers. When a transport was brought in and the outer doors of the gas chambers were opened, the Germans would knock on the windows shouting—*Dentisten raus!* (Dentists out!). Depending on the size of the transport, one or more groups of six men would go out to work. With pliers in their hands they would position themselves along the path on which the corpses were carried from the ramp to one or more of the mass graves. (When they began to incinerate the dead, they were carried to the ovens.)

It is worth mentioning that at the time when I began working in the death camp, there were two gassing structures in operation. The larger one had ten chambers, into each of which as many as four hundred people could enter. Each chamber was 7 metres long by 7 metres wide. People were stuffed into them like herrings. When one chamber was full, the second was opened, and so on. Small transports were brought to the smaller structure, which had three gas chambers, each of which could hold 450 to 500 persons. In that structure the gassing would last about twenty minutes, while in the more recent structure it would last about three quarters of an hour.

On days when the gentlemen would learn by telephone from the extermination headquarters in Lublin that no new transports would be arriving the next day, the murderers, out of sadism, would let the people stand stuffed into the gas chambers so that they would be asphyxiated. Once they stood like that for forty-eight hours and when the exterior doors were opened, a few people were still struggling and showing signs of life.

Most of the people were entirely swollen and black. The SS men or the Ukrainians would look in through the peep-holes to see if everyone was dead and if the rear doors could now be opened.

As I am standing at work at the table and beginning to get the hang of using the tools, we hear the above-mentioned knocking at our windows. Our group leader already has noticed that the ramp is starting to work, that the special ramp commando is about to open the doors. He appoints six men to go out onto the path where the carriers run with the corpses. He has included me in the group.

Each member of the group takes along two pairs of pliers. We then go outside to the transport. From the carpentry workshop, where among the carpenters is Yankl Wiernik (a Treblinka survivor whose "A Year in Treblinka" was published in New York in 1944 by Unser Tsait), each one of us grabs a bowl. In our shed there is no room for the bowls, so they are kept in the carpenters' room. A whole stack of them lies there. Each of us grabs a little water at the well and runs to work.

At the open space in front of the ramp the scene is an inferno. The rear door has been opened. When it is opened, deadly gas fumes are emitted from inside. The corpses, all standing, are so tightly pressed together and have their hands and feet so intertwined that the ramp commando are in danger of their lives until they are able to pull out the first few dozen corpses. The bodies then become looser and the corpses start to fall out by themselves. The tight compression sometimes results from the fact that people are terrorized and crammed in as they are driven into the gas chambers, so that everyone has to hold his breath in order to be able to find a bit of space. During their death agonies from asphyxiation the bodies also become swollen, and so the corpses form literally a single mass.

There was a difference in the appearance of the dead from the small and from the large gas chambers. In the small chambers death was easier and quicker. The faces often looked as if the people had fallen asleep, their eyes closed. Only the mouths of some of the gassed victims were distorted with a bloody foam visible on their lips. The bodies were covered in sweat. Before dying, people had urinated and defecated. The corpses in the larger gas chambers, where death took longer, were horribly deformed, their faces all black as if burned, the bodies swollen and blue, the teeth so tightly clenched that it was literally impossible to open them, and to get to the gold crowns we had sometimes to pull out the natural teeth—otherwise the mouth would not open.

The work of clearing out the corpses was divided up. In addition to the "ramp men" (about twenty men), forty to fifty carriers were employed, six "dentists" and, at the pits, a commando of grave-diggers. About ten of the latter stood in the pit and worked at laying out the corpses head to foot and foot to head so that the maximum number went in. A second group covered the corpses with sand, whereupon a second layer was laid down.

The pits were dug by a bulldozer (later on there were three of them). The pits were enormous, about 50 metres long, about 30 wide and several storeys deep. I estimate that the pits could contain about four storeys.

The movement, the running and chasing, the beatings at work constituted an infernal vicious circle. Over every group of workers stood several Germans or Ukrainians with whips in their hands, ceaselessly beating the Jews on their heads, backs, stomachs, hands, not much caring where the blows landed. If they did pay attention to the blows, it was to land them in a spot where it would hurt the most or where it could injure the body the most. The ramp men, the carriers and indeed everyone had to do their work at a fiendishly rapid tempo. The ramp men had to make sure that there was always a ready pile of corpses so that the carriers would not have to wait. The carriers had to grab a corpse on the run (picking out a lighter specimen from afar), throw it on the litter and gallop with it to the pit.

The litters were in the shape of a ladder with a strap to pull over the shoulders. The "dentists" stood in a row on the way from the ramp to the pit. The first in line had the function of quickly inspecting the mouth of the corpse, and, if he noticed gold or false teeth, of passing the corpse to one of the "dentists" down the line whose hands were free. The carriers stood aside for a moment, in order not to interfere with the operation. It was not permitted to lay a corpse on the ground. The carriers then held the corpse and the "dentist" quickly seized the tooth or bridge with his pliers and extracted it as fast as possible. Careful attention had to be paid not to miss a tooth that ought to have been extracted. At the pit the Germans would look and inspect. Woe to the "dentist" who had left a gold tooth in the mouth of a corpse.

I once experienced a case when a German noticed a gold tooth sparkling in the mouth of a corpse. Since I was the last one standing in the row of "dentists," the blame fell on me. I had to jump into the pit at once, rolling head over heels several times. I had to extract the tooth quickly, and when I climbed out again the SS man ordered me to stretch out on the ground and administered twenty-five lashes. Another time, somewhat later, I missed a whole mouthful of teeth. Once again I was the last one in the row. All the other "dentists" were busy, the corpse was very heavy, and the carriers who were hauling it thought they could throw it into the pit without it being inspected. Standing at his post at that time was *Unterscharführer* Gustav. He noticed unextracted teeth in the mouth of the corpse and thereupon the same scene was repeated. This time I received perhaps seventy lashes. He beat me on my back with all his strength, always in the same spot. He nearly severed my spinal cord. When with great difficulty I got up, blood was pouring over my body and into my trousers. On my back there was a big crust of blood; the next day it became apparent that I had blood poisoning. I would undoubtedly have died from it if not for Dr. Zimmermann, who operated on me. It was my good fortune that it was a Sunday, when we were free from work. Dr. Zimmermann had all his tools with him and performed the operation in the barracks, even with anesthesia. He opened the wound and cleaned it out, and in this way saved my life.

Chapter Ten

❦

*The Jews of Ostrowiec are driven into the gas
chambers at night.*

They resist.

The astonishment of Chief Mathias.

A new form of entertainment.

People strive to get into the gas chambers.

U NTIL 15 DECEMBER [1942] THE TRANSPORTS arrived regularly, approximately ten thousand people a day. If a transport arrived after 6:00 in the evening, its passengers were not gassed that day. The transport was kept at Treblinka station and only on the next day was it brought into the camp.

As it happened, on 10 December a transport of Jews from Ostrowiec was waiting at the station. The camp administration received the announcement that the next morning a new transport would be brought to Treblinka. The Commandant gave the order that the Jews of Ostrowiec should be brought in at night. The order was carried out. By then we were locked in our barracks and could see nothing. We only heard the usual screams. But when we went out to work the next morning, we saw the traces of the events of the previous night. The ramp men opened the rear doors and began to pull out the corpses. The carriers carried them to the pits. But this time the carriers and cleaning crew of the so-called *Schlauch* commando had an additional task.

The whole corridor of the structure with the three smaller gas chambers was filled with dead bodies. The floor was covered with dried blood, which reached to the ankles. We learned from the Ukrainians what had happened there. A group of about ten men who were being driven into the chambers refused to go. They resisted and, naked as they were, defended themselves with their fists and did not allow themselves to be shoved into the chambers. Thereupon the SS men opened fire on them with automatic weapons, killing them on the spot.

The ramp men carried out the corpses, the cleaning crew washed down the corridor, the painters as always whitewashed the walls that had been covered with the blood and brains of the dead, and the building once again stood ready to receive new victims.

Afterwards the Section Leader, Mathias, came over to us, the "dentists," and called out to our group leader, Dr. Zimmermann—Did you know, Doctor, that those chaps tried to swindle us?

Mathias was truly astonished and surprised. He could not grasp why the Jews did not willingly want to let themselves be murdered. He found this an abnormal development.

That day was extraordinarily difficult. Soon after the first transport a second one arrived, and, as it happened, in that transport there were many gold and false teeth to extract.

After a certain number of corpses had been dealt with, the teeth were collected in two bowls, and two dentists would take them to the well and wash them before bringing them into our shed to be worked on. In our shed there was always a supply of teeth stored in chests, and if we had not cleaned them of blood and of the bits of flesh that stuck to them, they would begin to stink.

When there was a short pause in the work, when the cleaning crew had finished in one of the gas chambers but the second one was not yet done gassing and the victims inside still showed signs of life or one could still hear their screams, the beasts forced us to dance and sing songs to the accompaniment of the Jewish orchestra that stood next to our barracks and played without interruption.

In December the transports grew less frequent. Some of the Germans were on leave. Mathias had left even earlier and did not return till after New Year's 1943. When he came back he looked much worse than he had before. It seems he felt better in Treblinka than he did at home. The air of Treblinka suited him. During the two days of Christmas there were no transports at all.

The transports began to arrive regularly once more around 10 January. That was a very difficult day. On that day fresh transports arrived. At the same time a "guest" came to us from Camp 1, *Obersturmführer* Franz, who was nicknamed "Lyalke" (Doll). Together with him came his dog, Barry, who was just as notorious as his master.

Once work had resumed, the Germans began to apply new methods.

Around 10 January, transports began arriving from the borderlands of eastern Poland, from Bialystok, Grodno and the surrounding areas. It was a hard winter with freezing temperatures. Now the sadists thought up a new form of entertainment. At a temperature of -20 Celsius they would keep rows of naked young women outdoors, not allowing them to enter the gas chambers. The men and the older women having already been asphyxiated, the rows of young women, half frozen, stood barefoot in the snow and ice, trembling, weeping, clinging to one another and begging in vain to finally be allowed into that "warmth" where death awaited them.

The Ukrainians and Germans looked on with pleasure and mockery at the pain of the young bodies, joking and laughing, until at last they mercifully allowed them to enter the "baths." Such scenes were repeated in the following days and continued throughout the winter.

It is worth mentioning that in winter the extraction of teeth became much more difficult. Whether it was because the corpses froze when the doors were opened, or the result of the freezing of the victims on the way to the gas chambers, the opening of their clenched mouths was fiendishly difficult for us. The more we struggled, the more the murderers knocked us over and beat us.

In general, even in summer, the victims tried to arrive at the gas chambers as quickly as they could during the final passage along the *Schlauch*. The gas chambers offered protection from the beatings, and people wanted to get everything over with as quickly as possible.

In February 1943 great piles of ash began to accumulate as a result of the decision to begin burning the corpses. A special ash commando was organized. In the morning, when everyone went out to work, the carriers, who worked in stages, would put the ashes from the furnace grills into crates that were attached to the litters. (These crates were also used when corpses taken from the pits to be incinerated were in such a state of decomposition that they could not be placed on the ladder-shaped litters but had to be thrown piece by piece into the crates.) The carriers dumped the ashes in piles, and it was at these piles that the specially organized ash commando now worked. The work of the ash commando was as follows:

The body parts of the corpses that had been incinerated in the ovens often kept their shape. It was not uncommon to take out whole charred heads, feet, bones etc. The workers of the ash commando then had to break up these body parts with special wooden mallets, which recalled the iron mallets used to pound gravel on motorways. Other instruments also resembled the tools used when working with sand and stone. Near the heaps of ash stood thick, dense wire meshes, through which the broken-up ashes were sifted, just as sand is sifted from gravel. Whatever did not pass through was beaten once more. The beating took place on sheet metal, which lay nearby. The carriers were not allowed to bring bones from the grills that had not been completely incinerated. They remained lying next to the furnaces and were thrown on top of the next layer of corpses that were brought in. The definitive "finished" ash had to be free of the least bit of bone and as fine as cigarette ash.

When great piles of this kind of finished ash had accumulated, the Germans began to carry out various experiments with a view to getting rid of the ash and erasing every trace of the murders that had taken place. They tried in the first instance to convert the ash into "earth" with the help of special liquids. Experts arrived and, standing over the ash heaps, mixed the ashes with sand in various proportions. Then they poured in some sorts of liquids out of bottles. But the results did not satisfy them. After the experiments they decided to bury the ash deep in the ground under thick layers of sand.

A shallow layer of ash was poured into the deep pits from which the corpses had been exhumed, then on top of that a shallow layer of sand, and so forth until they had reached the level of about 2 meters below the surface. The last 2 meters were filled only with sand. In this way they reckoned that they would erase forever the traces of their horrible crimes.

The Jewish workers who were employed in the emptying of the pits nevertheless used every opportunity to leave behind in the earth some remains of human bones. Since the pits became narrower as they grew deeper, and the earth along the sides would crumble, every time the Germans and their informers were absent the workers would bury as many bones as they could beneath a layer of sand.

The ash was poured in shallow layers—a layer of ash and a layer of sand. That was the usual procedure. The carriers who delivered the ash and sand from morning till night firmly tamped down the surface with their feet.

I remember that every morning when we went out to work, we would notice that the surfaces of the pits had burst in dozens of places. By day the ground was firmly trodden down, but at night the blood pressed up to the surface. This raised the level to such an extent that in the morning the carriers sweated with exertion while descending into the pits with their loads of ash and sand.

The blood of tens of thousands of victims, unable to rest, thrust itself upwards to the surface.

Chapter Eleven

⁂

Obersturmführer Franz and his dog Barry.

The murderers drink to the arrival of the British Jews.

A new "specialist."

I T IS A BEAUTIFUL DAY. THE MURDERERS ARE IN A good mood. Our Chief, Mathias, sits down on an embankment, and, along with him, his distinguished guest, Deputy Commandant *Obersturmführer* Franz, whom we call "Lyalke" (Doll). This Lyalke is a terrible murderer. His appearance at the open space in the camp triggers extraordinary fear. His specialty is slapping. From time to time he calls a worker over, tells him to stand at attention and gives him a powerful slap on his cheek. The victim then has to fall down and immediately get up, in order to receive a slap on the other cheek. Then he calls over his dog, Barry, who is almost as big as a man, and shouts—Man, bite that dog!—The dog is very obedient to his friend the Deputy Commandant and attacks the Jew.

Our Chief, Mathias, invites the criminal to sit down for a while and observe how well the work is proceeding. Lyalke sits down, and they converse, smiling.

They are in a good mood and pleased that the work is moving along at a brisk pace.

Their hearts swell with pride as they watch the living corpses running without interruption, like demons. Everyone is at his post and in fact when they are not present the work goes even better than usual. Their collaborators flog with their whips ceaselessly, ceaselessly . . .

The murderers are content. Our Chief orders a Ukrainian to bring him a good bottle of cognac from the canteen. It doesn't take long before his wish is fulfilled. They fill the first goblet, and the guest, Lyalke, says—We drink to the imminent arrival of the real Jews of England!

The Section Leader is very pleased with the joke and laughs—*Ja, das ist gut, das kommt sicher!* (Yes, that's good, that's sure to happen!)

In winter the criminals leave the women destined for the gas chambers outside at a temperature of -25 degrees Celsius. The snow is half a metre high and the murderers laugh—How beautiful it is!

In December 1942 the criminals began to set up ovens to burn the corpses, but they did not work well, as the corpses refused to burn. For that reason a crematorium was built with special fittings. A special motor was attached that increased the flow of air, and in addition a lot of petrol was poured in. But the corpses still do not want to burn well. The maximum number of incinerated corpses reaches a thousand per day. The murderers are not satisfied with this small quantity.

We wondered, unable to understand, why the murderers had begun to look for ways to burn the corpses of the people they had gassed. After all, we had kept on digging deeper and deeper pits, but now the tactics had changed. By pure chance we found out the reason: one of the murderers gave us a present of a piece of bread wrapped in newspaper. That was an extraordinary event for us. From the articles in the newspaper we learned that the German authorities had finally discovered, in Katyn, near Smolensk, the graves of ten thousand Polish officers who supposedly had been murdered by the Soviets. We understood that the murderers wanted to blacken the face of Soviet Russia and were therefore starting to burn the corpses so there no trace of what they had been doing would remain.

In January [1943] a new specialist came to our camp. We nicknamed him "Artist," since he plays his role so well. He is an extraordinary disposer of corpses. From the first moments of his arrival he is to be found at the pits. He laughs at the sight of them and is happy and satisfied with his role.

After a few days he gets to work intensively. He orders the ovens to be dismantled and laughs at how the existing ones have been installed. He assures our Chief that from now on the work will go much better. He lays down ordinary long, thick iron rails to a length of 30 metres. Several low walls of poured cement are built to a height of 50 centimetres. The width of the oven is a meter and a half. Six rails are laid down, no more. He orders that the first layer of corpses should consist of women, especially fat women, placed with their bellies on the rails. After that anything that arrives can be laid on top: men, women, children. A second layer is placed on top of the first, the pile growing narrower as it rises, up to a height of 2 metres.

The corpses are thrown up by a special commando called the Fire Commando. Two fire-workers catch every corpse that is brought to them by the corpse carriers. One catches a hand and foot on one side, the second catches the other side, and then they throw the dead person into the oven. In this way some twenty-five hundred corpses are piled on. Then the "specialist" orders dry twigs placed underneath and lights them with a match. After a few minutes the fire flares up so strongly that it is difficult to get any closer to the oven than 50 metres. The first fire is lit, and the test is successful. The camp administration shows up, and all of them shake the hand of the inventor. But he is not pleased with the fact that for the time being only one oven is working. Therefore he orders that the excavator that was used to dig the graves should now start digging out the corpses that have been lying in the ground for months . . .

The excavator starts to dig out the dead—hands, feet, heads separately. The Artist, being a specialist, orders the machine operators to dump the remains in a circle so that the carriers with their litters (these are now different litters, box-like in shape, so that nothing will fall out of them while running fast) can quickly run over, grab the human body parts with their hands, throw them into the litters and quickly carry them to the ovens.

The work is now even harder than before. The stench is terrible. The workers are sprayed with the fluid that trickles from the cadavers. Often the excavator driver deliberately heaves the body parts onto the workers and bloodies them. It sometimes happens that our Chief, seeing that a worker is lying bloodied on the ground, asks him the cause. When he answers that he was injured by the excavator while dumping the cadavers, he receives several lashes as well.

But the Artist walks around half-mad with rage, because the work still is not proceeding as well as he would like it to.

Soon afterwards, two new excavators are brought into the camp. The joy of the murderers knows no limits, since now the work will proceed *taddellos* (flawlessly). The next day all the excavators began to function. For us this is simply hell, since the same number of workers now have to serve three corpse processors. Each time, the machines throw out dozens of corpses and we have to carry them immediately to the oven.

The criminal specialist also introduces a modification of the work. He creates a special commando of several workers whose job consists of tossing the dead onto the carriers' litters. He does this so that the carriers will not have to deposit the litters on the ground and in the process waste several minutes. The throwers fill the litters, throwing the body parts of the dead with pitchforks so that the carriers, who pick up their litters in the morning, will have no possibility to rest for a moment until evening.

It turns out that the corpses dug out of the pits burn even better than those of recently gassed people. Every day new ovens are constructed, more and more of them. After a few days there are six ovens. Each oven is served by several workers who load it with fodder.

The Artist is still not satisfied. He sees that the work is hampered by the intense fire, which does not let anyone get close to the oven. The work plan is therefore changed. The ovens are loaded by day and are lit at 5:30 in the evening.

Chapter Twelve

❧

About 250,000 corpses are burned.

Transports of Jews from Bulgaria.

The music plays . . .

It is March 1943. The work proceeds ever faster. The Chief orders that the excavators should be ready two hours before roll call, so that we won't have to wait. One grave after another is cleared. If a pit has been cleared but a pool of blood has collected in a corner, a worker had to strip naked, descend into the pit, and scour the pit with his hands, looking for remaining human body parts.

From day to day the work improves. The ovens are moved from place to place, closer to the pits, so that the path is shorter and less time is wasted. It once happened that an oven was brought next to a huge grave, where perhaps a quarter of a million people were buried. As usual the oven was loaded with the proper number of bodies and in the evening it was lit. But a strong wind carried the fire over to the huge grave and engulfed it in flames. The blood of some quarter of a million people began to flare, and thus burned for a night and a day. The whole camp administration came to look upon this marvel, gazing with satisfaction at the blaze. The blood came up to the surface and burned as if it were fuel.

I remember 29 March. This day has remained etched in my memory: our comrade Yankl from Czestochowa lay down to sleep and did not wake up in the morning. Each of us wished for such good fortune. We accompanied him to the flames, threw him onto the burning corpses and cremated him.

It has been raining since morning without interruption. But we have to work. Each of us is soaked. The murderers take cover under the eaves and shout to us from there—Faster, keep up the pace! From time to time an SS man runs over and whips us. Although the soil is sandy it turns muddy, and it becomes hard for us to run. The Chief orders us to bring several dozen litters of ash from the ovens and spread it on the ground. The mud absorbs the human blood. From time to time we have to add ashes, because it keeps raining harder. The day weeps along with us.

Since three excavators are in operation, the carriers are divided into three groups. It sometimes happens that one excavator breaks down and it takes several minutes to fix it. We likewise come to a halt. The Artist appears and good-naturedly inquires why we are standing around doing nothing while at the ovens there is a great deal of ash that needs to be carried away. Our group foreman points out that the excavator will soon be repaired. The Artist answers that we will have time to carry away at least one voluntary round of ashes (he calls it an *Ehren-Runde*).

The month of April began with fresh transports from abroad, especially Bulgaria.

In the early hours the Chief appears, orders the gas chambers to be shut and tells us that if we work well we will be fed well. Not long afterward we again hear cries of "Help, help" and "*Shema yisrael.*" After a few minutes, the cries from the gas chambers are silenced, and after half an hour—newly gassed people.

I look at the gassed people: they look very different from us. It's as if they had been specially selected for their youth and beauty. I had seldom seen among our Jews such healthy, beautiful bodies. Even after being gassed they look as if they were still alive, but asleep.

They were brought here in special Pullman cars. They even brought furniture with them, and a lot of food. Until the last minute they believed that they were being resettled in Russia for work. Their valuables were taken away from them and put in the so-called "deposit." The people, seeing that all the valuables were being thrown onto a single pile, pointed out that mistakes would be made when retrieving the objects after the bath, since no notes were being made of what belonged to whom. Yes, the murderers already knew to whom the things would belong—to the *Herrenvolk*, the master race.

We learned from some workers from Camp 1 that when the transport of Bulgarian Jews arrived, music was playing. The Jews were convinced that nothing bad would happen to them. As they exited the train, they asked if this was the big industrial complex Treblinka . . .

The SS man Karl Spetzinger appears and warns us "dentists" that we should pay close attention, because almost every one of the Bulgarians has false teeth.

We find it difficult to cope, since in fact each one of them has a mouth full of false teeth. We have to pull, and the carriers weep because the corpses are exceptionally heavy. The murderers are beside themselves because the "dentists" detain almost every corpse. They start beating us. The Chief declares that if the "shit" is not removed by 4:00 in the afternoon, we will get no food. That day we work without food as a punishment.

A few minutes after 4:00 there remains no trace of the young and beautiful Bulgarian Jews.

Chapter Thirteen

❦

An even bigger oven is built.
Several days without transports.
News of the revolt in the Warsaw Ghetto.
The traces of murder are effaced.
The earth is planted with lupins.
Himmler's visit to Treblinka

IN THE SECOND HALF OF APRIL THE STAFF APPEARS with our Chief, Mathias, at its head. We see that they have brought plans with them, and at the same time they measure a section of terrain a few metres from the ten big gas chambers. The next morning several workers are chosen, and under the command of an SS man they begin to dig several metres from the gas chambers. It turns out that they are starting to build a much bigger and stronger oven right next to the gas chambers, in order to be able to burn the corpses at once. This work goes on for ten days. Apparently they are expecting many transports. By now we have arrived at the last days of April and the oven is still not ready. The Chief orders that a new oven be erected close to the gas chambers in a few days. The gas chambers are sealed in preparation. But the day is a happy one for us, because no transports arrive. We notice how the murderers run around like mad dogs; they beat, they scream like scalded pigs.

In the evening we heard the whistle of a locomotive. But it turned out that it was a freight train. Another day went by and no transports arrived. The murderers are furious. We are unable to find out what has happened. Three days pass in this way. On the third day the Chief orders the gas chambers reopened. For the first time in Treblinka it happened that the gas chambers were sealed in readiness but no transports came.

In a few days the chambers were sealed again and a few days later a transport came. Almost all of the murderers were present to receive the arrivals. Each of them has a whip in his hand, and Ivan holds his three-metre-long bar.

I am in the dentists' shed. I hear the pitiful screams. The murderers are wild. They have selected three women from the transport to work in the laundry. We believe that they deliberately sent the women to us so that we would know what happened to the Jews of Warsaw.

The three women were in a daze for three days and did not understand what we said to them. After a few days they calmed down a bit and told us that the Jews of Warsaw resisted heroically and did not let themselves be killed off, that the Ghetto is in flames and the Jews are fighting with weapons in their hands.

It saddens us to hear from the women that the Ghetto is in flames. But the women are proud when they tell how the Jews fought and that there were German casualties as well.

We are heartbroken by the news, but at the same time the will and determination rose up within us to free ourselves from Treblinka.

The work proceeds at a rapid pace. It seems as if they have a particular deadline by which everything here should be liquidated. No sooner is one pit emptied than the next one is dug.

The Artist, seeing that there are still whole corpses in the upper layers of the mass graves, gives orders to drop the litters, pick up the corpses by hand and burn them in the ovens. Each carrier tries to utilize the moment when the machine descends into the pit to run over, grab a corpse and run away again, thereby avoiding being hit by the falling corpses that the excavator throws up.

The corpses are counted by special workers. Every evening they have to report to Chief Mathias how many corpses were burned. Only whole corpses are counted—those which still have the head attached. If the head is missing, the corpse does not count. Heads are counted separately. The Chief is under the impression that he is being cheated, that the counting is not being carried out correctly. He beats the workers and threatens to have them shot.

We "dentists" have a lot of work. There are several big chests filled with teeth. We have to clean them and every couple of days deliver a suitcase of dental gold, other gold and precious stones.

From time to time we receive visits from the Commandant of Treblinka. He speaks calmly and requests of our foreman that if we find a big, beautiful stone, we should give it directly to him. (Normally Chief Mathias takes such items to the camp coffers. The gold and valuables are sent, we have heard, directly to the Reischsbank in Berlin, where the human dental gold is smelted into ingots.) The Commandant, however, wishes to have such a stone for his own house museum as a souvenir . . . His request is easily fulfilled, since we are used to giving such stones to his assistants, hoping thereby to avoid extra beatings.

From time to time it happens that one of the murderers brings us a loaf of bread or a few cigarettes, which are then divided into twenty parts.

In May a new SS man arrives, and on the following day he comes into the "dentists'" shed to have his wristwatch repaired. A worker among us is a watchmaker by trade and fixes his watch. Our foreman takes advantage of the opportunity to ask for several suitcases from Camp 1. The SS man promises, not knowing that no one from Camp 1 is allowed to come here. In the afternoon the German returns in the company of a worker from Camp 1, bringing several suitcases. He wants to send the worker back, but right from the start he is detained by Chief Mathias, who glares at the SS man and berates him for not knowing that no one from Camp 1 is allowed to come here. He tells the worker to turn around, undress and go down into the pit, where he shoots him.

In June fewer transports arrive than ever before. The new oven is ready. Corpses are thrown in as quickly as possible. The work of clearing out the pits likewise proceeds at a rapid pace. Ten pits have already been entirely cleaned out. The last, the eleventh, pit is one of the four biggest, where a total of a quarter of a million people lie. Two excavators work at this pit. A special commando is created, called the *Knochen-Kolonne* (Bone Brigade). Their task is to walk around with a bucket and pick up the tiniest bones, so that no trace will remain. The Supervisor points out that if the greatest care is not taken, it will be considered sabotage. What that means does not have to be explained to any of us.

The third excavator, which is not in use for digging up corpses, begins to move earth from one place to another. Several workers assigned to the excavator have to keep an eye out for bones or other body parts and immediately bring them to the oven. The earth is turned over twice, so that no trace should remain.

By the end of June the space of the eleven pits, where hundreds of thousands of bodies had lain, was completely cleared. The earth was smoothed out and sown with lupins.

It soon became clear—the murderers had a deadline: 1 July for Camp 1. We learned that that day we were to expect a notable guest—Himmler. Great preparations were made to receive him. The work was completed two days ahead of schedule.

It is the first of July. We were supposed to work in the afternoon. At the last minute, however, work was called off.

We lie confined to our barracks and see through the little windows that a strong guard has been placed around the building. A few minutes later Himmler arrives with his entourage. They inspect the gas chambers and head for the open space, which by then has been made neat and clean. Himmler apparently is satisfied. He smiles, and his accomplices beamed with joy.

Several shots are heard—a signal of victory.

It is worth mentioning that among the SS men in Treblinka there were some who had come from the working class, former members of the Communist Party. One SS man was a former Evangelical pastor.

Chapter Fourteen

❦

It was a hot day . . . "Trinkets."
Mikolai and Ivan.
The murderer "Tsik-Tsak."

I T WAS A HOT DAY. SEVERAL STAFF MEMBERS, WHO HAD gone on leave a fortnight earlier, had returned to the camp though every one of these bandits receives twenty-four days of leave every six weeks because of their strenuous "work." While on leave, they had dressed in civilian clothes and left their sacred uniforms in the camp. When they came back from their *Erholung* (recuperation) they were constantly in a bad mood. We once overheard a conversation in which one of them told the other that the city he comes from was being bombed day and night and that there were many casualties from the air raids. We also notice that the murderers, coming back from leave, don't look good. It appears that the care they get at home is not as good as what they get in Treblinka. Here, in Treblinka, they can afford everything, since there is no lack of money. After all, each victim who arrives in Treblinka have managed to bring something with him or her.

It is a very difficult day today. SS man *Unterscharführer* Chanke—we call him The Whip because he is a specialist in beating—is in a bad mood. His comrade *Unterscharführer* Loeffler is no small sadist himself. He has terrifying eyes, and all of us are afraid that his glance will fall on us because in that case we are done for. Despite the fact that they are tired from their journey, they beat us mercilessly.

I remember a case in which two workers forgot themselves and placed the corpses of three small children on the litter instead of one adult corpse. *Unterscharführer* Loeffler detained them, covered them with blows from his whip and screamed—You dogs, why are you carrying trinkets? ("Trinkets" is what they called little children.)

The "trinket"-bearers had to run back and collect an adult corpse.

On such a hot day the Ukrainian henchmen feel very good. They work left and right with their whips. Mikolai and Ivan, who work as mechanics on the motor that sends the gas into the chambers and also work on the generator that provides electric lighting for Treblinka, feel happy and in splendid shape in such weather. Ivan is about twenty years old and looks like a giant healthy horse. He is pleased when he has an opportunity to let off his energy on the workers. From time to time he feels the urge to take a sharp knife, detain a worker who is running past and cut off his ear. The blood spurts, the worker screams, but he must keep running with his litter. Ivan waits calmly until the worker runs back and orders him to put the litter down. He then tells him to strip and go over to the pit, where he shoots him.

Ivan once came over to the well where I and another "dentist" called Finkelstein were washing teeth. Ivan was carrying an auger. He ordered Finkelstein to lie down on the ground and drilled the iron tool into his buttocks. That was meant to be a joke. The wretched victim did not even scream out loud, only groaned. Ivan laughed and shouted repeatedly—Lie still, otherwise I'll shoot you!

Among the faithful Ukrainian helpers there are several heroes of this type.

Etched in my memory is the Ukrainian we called "Zacke-Zacke" because when beating people he always yelled—*Zacke, zacke*! (roughly: Pow, pow!). He has a special whip that is longer than all the other whips. Today Zacke-Zacke is on duty. He has special privileges. He chooses the gate as his post. Here the entrance is narrow and it is convenient for him to beat people because he has everyone in his sight and it is impossible to avoid him. Zacke-Zacke is wild. Sweat pours down his diabolical face. The workers cry and he beats. In such cases Dr. Zimmermann, who knew Russian, would try to distract him. Sometimes that was the only remedy that would cause him to forget beating people for a while.

After the episode with Loeffler and the auger, Finkelstein had to get up and go back to work. He was a healthy young man. At the first opportunity Dr. Zimmermann took him into his room and washed and bandaged his wound. The wound healed; Finkelstein survived till the revolt.

Chapter Fifteen

❧

Life in the barracks.
The typhus epidemic.
The Lazarett

OUR LIFE IS DIFFICULT AND FILTHY. WE WORK FROM 6:00 in the morning until 6:00 in the evening. After work we are so tired that we fall to the ground exhausted. Not even a drop of water is to be had in the barracks, because the well is far away in the open space and after work we are driven into the dirty barracks, which is surrounded by barbed wire. Around it stands a special watch to guard us.

Treblinka is guarded by 144 Ukrainians and about a hundred SS men. They keep an eye on us like precious jewels. We are counted three times a day. But although every one of us is bruised and battered and every part of our bodies ache, not one of us dares to report himself sick. It often happens that the newly arrived workers don't know that you must not be sick and must never report during roll call that you are ill. They are ordered to step out of line and undress on the spot. The murderers force them to do punishment exercises while naked, and then they are shot.

In Treblinka you must not be sick. Many of us cannot endure it and commit suicide. That is an ordinary event here. Every morning we notice that there are people hanging in the barracks.

I recall a father and son who had been in this hell for two days. They decided to commit suicide. Having only one strap between them, they agreed that the father would hang himself first and after that the son would take him down and use the same strap to hang himself, and that was exactly how it happened. In the morning both were dead and we carried them out so that the chief murderer could verify that the number was correct.

It sometimes happens that as many as seventy workers are brought to us from a new transport. They work for a few hours until roll call. The next day, at roll call, they report that they are sick. The Chief assigns them to carry corpses. He hurries them along and makes them carry three corpses instead of one. They have to run fast, in step, and at the same time are brutally beaten on their heads. They are so exhausted that they cannot remain upright. After half an hour they are told to undress and are beaten some more. The murderers scream—You dogs, you don't want to work! Then they order them to go over to the pit into which the corpses of the victims of gassing are thrown. Each of the murderers wants to have the privilege of shooting. They agree among themselves that each of them should shoot several people.

They are pleased with this amusement and aim at the head. Seldom do two bullets have to be used for one victim.

In the early days, few of us knew each other, since every day new people arrived to take the place of those who had been shot. Later the murderers changed their tactics. Shooting workers soon after their arrival meant that the work went badly, since no-one had time to become accustomed to it.

We live here in great filth. We wear our blood-covered shoes and clothes by day and by night we put them under our heads. We sleep crowded together, each one pressed against his neighbour. We have been wearing the same shirts we came here with and are covered with vermin. It is impossible to wash a shirt. The criminals shipped hundreds of wagons of clothing out of here, and we have nothing to wear. We suffer greatly from hunger. We receive only a small part of the food that the Jews brought with them. It reaches the point that the workers, finding a piece of bread in the chambers after the people have been gassed, do not hesitate to eat it.

In the middle of the twelfth month the work becomes more irregular. Fewer transports arrive and the work goes more slowly. Many of the SS men are on leave. At the same time a typhus epidemic breaks out in the camp, and many of the workers go around with a fever of 40 degrees Celsius. They can hardly stand, but are afraid to report that they are sick.

At a roll-call, the Deputy Chief of the Camp, Karl Spetzinger (an SS man with the rank of *Scharführer*), announces that anyone who is sick can report to the doctor and nothing bad will happen to him. He will be able to remain in the barracks. At the same time he announces that the barracks located in the back row of the camp will be set up as a *Lazarett* (sick bay).

This arouses great fear, but nevertheless many people begin to report themselves as sick because they can no longer stand. Over the course of several days the sick bay fills up. The number of sick people reaches about a hundred. I am among them. We lie there, burning with fever. We receive no medical treatment. But it is good that we can lie there for a few days. The murderer has kept his word, just like all the criminal promises of the Germans.

After a few days, at 5:00 in the afternoon, several SS men give the order to expel ninety sick people from the *Lazarett*. The Ukrainians rush into the barracks and drag one person after another from their bunks by their feet. In about fifteen minutes the murderers have dragged out some eighty-odd sick people. They are not allowed to get dressed but take with them the blankets under which they were lying. Of about a hundred sick people, thirteen are left. The rest are driven to the open space. In a few minutes, the sound of guns is heard . . .

We, the remaining few, are convinced that the next day it will be our turn to be shot. We therefore report that we are now healthy, and the doctor orders that we be given underwear. Each of us has to strip and wash himself. The door and windows of the barracks are open, the temperature is 20 degrees below freezing, and we wash ourselves. I want to get dressed, but I cannot stand upright. The same is true of my comrades. It is 4:00 in the afternoon and at 6:00 we have to go for roll call. We are kept standing for an hour at roll call, during which time we have to sing. The greatest music-lover of them all is the murderer Karl Spetzinger. He also likes recitations. Our comrade Spiegel, a former actor from Warsaw, has to recite to the accompaniment of the camp orchestra.

After this amusement we are told—*Antreten! Rechts um!* (Fall in! Right turn!) We now also have to march in the open space. SS man Gustav, seeing that several comrades are barely able to walk, orders them to step out and shoots them. One of those called out, knowing what awaits him, steps out with a smile and bids us farewell in a loud voice—I hope that you all will live to see what I have not lived to see.

The murderer flies into a rage and shoots him at once.

I try my best to lift my feet high. With a song we march half-dead into the barracks.

As a result of the filth, scabies began to appear. Almost all of us became sick with it. Having no medicines, we used ordinary brine. From that we get boils all over our bodies. The pain is unbearable. But in Treblinka you had to bear and survive that too . . .

Chapter Sixteen

❦

We prepare for the revolt.
Passover in the barracks.
The revolt in Treblinka.

As has already been mentioned, in the most recent period workers have remained with us for longer than before. That has been a great stroke of luck for us. As a result, we have been able to get to know each other better. We have begun to trust one another more and to think about the possibilities of escape from here. We know that this is a difficult undertaking and are even afraid to discuss it among ourselves for fear of denunciation. We examine various possibilities. But the plans are difficult to carry out. We are unarmed and yet we plan all sorts of things. Our conversations take place in the corners of the barracks, and there is always a guard consisting of our own people to keep an eye out in case one of the murderers comes into the barracks.

In January 1943, fifteen workers from Camp 1 are brought to us. It often happens that instead of shooting people in Camp 1 they are brought to us to work with the corpses, which amounts to the same thing . . . a swift and certain death. Among the fifteen new workers, there are two, Adolf, a former sailor, and Zelo Bloch, a Czech Jew and an officer in the Czech army, who are devoted comrades. In a few days we become friends with them. They inform us that in Camp 1 they are planning a revolt. In that camp there are more possibilities, since a weapons store is located there. They therefore plan to make a copy of the key to the storeroom and steal weapons from there. These two comrades are very energetic, devoted and honest. They console us and begin to work intensively. We make every effort to establish contact with Camp 1. It is very difficult, but we make the most of the opportunity created by the fact that several of us work at the *Schlauch* cleaning off the blood of the murder victims. The *Schlauch* extends to the border of Camp 1, and there our people come in contact with the *Schlauch* workers from the other side. We succeed in reaching an understanding with them despite the fact that we are guarded by an SS man and a Ukrainian. Our method of communication is the following: a comrade speaks with another from our camp in a loud voice. The people from Camp 1 who are working nearby hear the conversation and respond in the same way—with a loud conversation among themselves. The criminals are particularly watchful to see that we do not speak to each other. I remember one case: after great effort we succeeded in persuading the Chief to allow several of our comrades who had brothers in Camp 1 to meet with them. His permission came with a warning: they can ask each other how they are. There can be no talking about work or about what our work consists of. The meeting took place in Camp 1. The conversations lasted at most for five minutes.

Our comrades came back content. Despite the fact that an SS man stood between each brother, and that they were only permitted to speak German, they were nevertheless able to bring back some important news. The news was the following: in Camp 1 they had made a copy of the key to the weapons store and soon they would begin the work of liberation.

Our joy was indescribable. We, the broken cripples, gained new strength, and each of us wanted to believe that we would succeed.

In the meantime the work continues. Fifteen Jewish women are brought to us from a transport from Bialystok. Some of them are to work in the kitchen, the rest in the laundry, which has been specially built. The sanitary conditions are being improved to a certain extent, and orders have been issued to give us a clean shirt every week, and warm water to wash with every Sunday. Life becomes a bit easier. At the same time a toilet is constructed, and a worker named Schwer, an engineer by profession, is assigned to it.

He is ordered to dress like a clown. He must wear a skullcap, a long black coat like a rabbi and a red scarf, and carry a black stick. In addition he has an alarm clock hung around his neck. This toilet supervisor is given the order that no one can spend longer than two minutes in his toilet. If anyone sits there longer, he will be whipped. The camp

Chief often hides in a corner to observe how long people are sitting in the toilet and if the Toilet Supervisor is admitting only those who have numbers. We had to have special numbers to go to the toilet, and it often happened that the bandits refused to issue the numbers. You could be close to bursting, but instead of a number you got the whip.

The murderers like to amuse themselves at the expense of the toilet supervisor. He is constantly given something new to wear so he will look even funnier. He must clean the toilet wearing a rabbi's clothes. In the evening at roll call he has to stand in his "uniform" and the murderers often ask him—Rabbi, how goes it with the shit?

He must answer—Very good!

The season of Passover is approaching. The murderers wish to turn it into a farce and give us flour for baking matzo and a bottle of wine. A seder is prepared and the SS men come to our barracks as guests. Among us there is a cantor from Warsaw who bakes the matzos and directs the seder. The murderers poke fun at this comedy and after a few minutes they leave the barracks.

I recall the night of the seder: several comrades performed the ceremony. Outside a breeze was blowing, the ovens were burning, and the flames were flaring. That evening ten thousand Jews were burning; in the morning no trace would be left of them. And we carried out the seder according to all the rules.

The next morning, as we were starting work, the oven specialist turned to us (as if anyone had asked him) and said that he knew very well that our work is very difficult and very dirty as well. So he pretended to ask us if we would like him to increase our number by fifty workers, thereby making our work easier. But he set the condition that we would receive the same food rations as before, which we would have to share with the new arrivals. He did not wait for our reply and said that he thought we would prefer to work a bit harder so long as our rations were not reduced. At the same time he assured us that it wouldn't be long before we were finished with this *Scheisse* and then life would be easier for us. Each of us would then receive a new set of clothes, and the work would become less arduous and more comfortable.

The next day we found out that what we were meant to have said was that the reward of a fine, clean life we would receive after removing the traces of their criminal activity would actually be our deaths. The bandit came to us yet again and explained yet again that nothing bad would happen to us. We listened yet again and thought of our freedom . . .

We decide together with the workers in Camp 1 to blow up the camp. Not everyone is told about this. The decision is kept secret. Only the leaders and those comrades who have been assigned special tasks know about it.

The plan of the revolt is as follows: everyone will work normally, very carefully, not revealing the least change in our routine or demeanor. Everyone knows what his responsibility is. In order to carry it out, each of us must place himself close to his appointed task. According to the plan, when we hear two shots coming from Camp 1 that will be the signal for the revolt. All of us are ready. Several comrades are assigned to set the gas chambers on fire. Others have the task of killing SS men and Ukrainians and seizing their weapons. Several men who work near the observation posts are to try and distract the Ukrainians there with pieces of gold.

All are at their assigned positions.

We, the "dentists," have the task of gathering as much gold as possible to take along with us. We plan, upon escaping from our camp, to head in the direction of the Treblinka Labour Camp, which lies 2 kilometres away, in order to liberate the Jews and Christians interned there.

The plans are all in place, but unfortunately there is an unforeseen change: on the day chosen for the uprising, a transport arrives at 5:00 in the morning, and with it many SS men and Ukrainians. This ruins our plans and we are forced to postpone our action. We cannot get over this disaster. The fear in Camp 1 is very great, because they now have to put back the weapons into the storehouse that were so difficult to steal. But they succeed in returning them and, happily, none of the murderers notice.

Difficult days begin for us. It is impossible to get anything done because we are surrounded by a strengthened watch.

In May the weather turns hot and the corpses being torn out of the ground cause the air to stink. The murderers cannot bring themselves to approach the pits. The excavator operators and SS men choke on the fetid air. They are forced to change the work schedule, and instead of working from 6:00 in the morning we now must begin at 4:00. The rollcall is at 3:30. We work until 2:00 in the afternoon without interruption. Then we receive the midday meal.

It often happens that we have to keep working during the afternoon because new transports arrive.

We are constantly being hurried at work. The pits are emptied more and more every day. We let the people in Camp 1 know that if they do not advance the date for the uprising, we will have to do it ourselves before it is too late. We are divided in our opinions. One group is in favour of blowing up the camp ourselves. The other group is certain that if we act alone we are doomed to failure.

We cannot wait any longer. Every day seems like a year. We decide to give Camp 1 the latest date we can accept, and if we do not get a clear answer from them with a concrete date for the revolt, we will not wait any longer, no matter the cirumcstance.

We receive from them only the answer that we should be patient and wait a few more days. Finally we receive a concrete reply from Camp 1: the uprising is set for 2 August, 4:30 in the afternoon. We wait impatiently for that day.

The morning of 2 August is beautiful. The sun is shining. All of us are feeling brave. Despite our fears, we are all happy that the time has come. There is a smile on everyone's face. We feel new strength, we feel more alive than ever. We go off to work with joy in our hearts, though we tell each other to try not to show it in our faces.

We prepare cans of benzine fuel, supposedly for the motors. Our barracks leader, who works in the camp as a butcher, turns to the Camp Deputy, Karl Spetzinger, for permission to sharpen his knives, because we are to receive a dead horse and the knives are dull. Spetzinger agrees, and Kalman the butcher sharpens his knives and the pliers to cut the barbed wire.

Everything is ready. Our excitement is running high, but so is our fear that the murderers might find out and shoot us. We step out for the midday meal. The latest news from Camp 1 is that everything is ready. Our only concern is that something might happen once again to spoil our plans. We have seen to it that at every point, such as the ovens, there will still be people at work, so that no one will be shut up in the barracks and unable to come to our aid. We claim that the fires need attention; that they are not burning well. In the kitchen we supposedly haven't drawn enough water so we have to send several people back to get more. These are in fact three good soldiers. Their task, the moment the revolt begins, will be to cut the throats of the Ukrainian guards and seize their weapons.

The midday rations are being distributed. We are all hungry, as always, but none of us is able to eat anything. No one asks for seconds of soup. Dozens of comrades do not touch the food. Afterwards all of us go back to work filled with happiness. We say to one another—*Ha-yom, ha-yom!*"(Hebrew: The Day, the Day!).

The work goes quickly. The murderers are pleased that the work is humming along. We avoid speaking to one another, so that no one will notice anything. Our tools are hidden in the appropriate places.

Our comrade Adolf, using various pretexts, tries to check every position. Despite all our preparations, there are still many among us who have no idea what is supposed to happen here. The time passes with extraordinary slowness. The fear that something may go wrong is unbearable.

The clock strikes 3:30.

We hear two shots from the direction of Camp 1—a sign that the revolt has started there. A few minutes later we receive the order to quit working. Everyone hurries to his post. A few seconds after that, flames engulf the gas chambers. They have been set on fire. The Ukrainian standing guard next to the barracks lies on the ground like a stuck pig, blood flowing from him, his weapon now being used by our comrade, Zelo. Shots are heard from all sides. The Ukrainians, whom our comrades have lured from the watchtowers, lie dead. Two SS excavator operators are dead. We head for the barbed wire shouting— *Revolutsya v Berline*! (Russian: Revolution in Berlin!). Several of the Ukrainians become disorientated and raise their hands. Their weapons are taken from them. We cut the wires one after the other. We are already at the third barbed-wire fence.

I am next to the barracks. Many comrades have become confused and are hiding inside out of fear. We urge them out, shouting—Comrades, come out to freedom, faster, faster!

All are now outside. The third fence has been cut open. Fifty metres further on there are trestles, thickly interwoven with barbed wire. We try to cut these as well.

The firing of the murderers' machine guns can be heard now. Some of them have succeeded in getting hold of their weapons. At the trestles lie many of our comrades who became entangled in the wires and were unable to escape.

I am among the last to go. I am already outside. Next to me is comrade Kruk, from Plock. He falls into my arms— Comrade, we are free. We kiss one another. I manage to run a few dozen metres when I see that the murderers are coming after us with machine guns. An automobile is bearing down on us at the same time. On the roof of the car is a machine gun shooting in all directions. Many fall down dead. There are dead bodies at every step. I change direction and run to the left off the road. The car continues along that Polish road and soon it is ahead of me. We run in various directions. The murderers pursue us from all sides.

I notice that the peasants working the fields and the shepherds run away out of fear. Finally, having run about 3 kilometres, we find ourselves in a small woodland area. We decide that there is no point in running further and hide in the dense brush. We number some twenty people. The group is too big, and we divide into two groups of ten men each. The groups are separated by about 150 metres.

We lie there for several minutes and suddenly see that Ukrainians with several SS men have surrounded the wood and are entering it. They encounter the second group and all of them are immediately shot.

Among us there is a Czech called Masaryk, a nephew of the former Czech President Masaryk. His wife was Jewish and he accompanied her to Treblinka. When he sees that the murderers are closing in on us, he takes a razor blade from his pocket and slits his wrists. Blood spurts from his wrists. I try to stop him, but he cannot be dissuaded, out of fear of falling yet again into the hands of the murderers.

We lie quietly for a brief period. Fortunately, they did not notice us and left the wood. I bind Masaryk's wrists with a bit of linen and succeed in stanching the flow of blood. We lie there for a time, then notice that civilians have entered the wood. They apparently have noticed us and have turned back towards us. We decide to run away quickly. We run for several hundred metres and come to another wood. Evening falls and it begins to turn dark. At midnight we proceed further, not knowing where we are going.

Masaryk, a former military officer, is able to orientate himself at night by the stars. With him leading the way, we move on. We walk all night. At sunrise we find ourselves in a big, dense forest. We decided to stay there all day. We are exhausted and very hungry.

We lie there a whole day. We take turns every few hours to make sure that no-one snores loudly if he falls asleep, since every rustle resounds in the forest.

Chapter Seventeen

We knock at a peasant's door.
The murderers look for us.
I head for Warsaw.
I meet a man.
They want to hand me over to the police.
I arrive in Warsaw

AT MIDNIGHT WE SET OFF AND LEAVE THE FOREST. The night is clear, and we realize that we are not very far from Treblinka. We roam around then return to the forest where we walk till morning. On the way we come across a muddy stream. Our comrade Masaryk crouches on all fours and drinks the muddy water. We do the same.

After three days of wandering, tired and hungry, we decide that we have to take a chance and go to a peasant's house to find out where we are and ask for something to eat.

I and my comrade Kalman, the one who set the gas chambers on fire, knock at a peasant's gate. The others remain hidden in the forest, afraid that we might encounter unfriendly people.

The peasant opens the gate but will not let us in. He tells us that Germans in automobiles and on bicycles have been looking for us all day long. At the same time we learn that the mayor has let it be known that any peasant who turns over a Jew to him or to the police will receive a big reward.

The peasant gives us a loaf of bread and some milk, asking for gold in exchange. We give him two watches. We learn that we are 15 kilometres from Treblinka. We want to find out if he knows where there are partisan units. He doesn't know, but he informs us that 5 kilometres from here there are big forests. We go in that direction and wander around for fourteen days. But we do not encounter any partisans. It often happens that when we knock at the gates of a peasant house, they refuse to open or to answer our questions. We are so weakened by hunger and thirst that we can hardly remain upright. We pull up potatoes and beets in the fields and eat them raw. Our situation is desperate. By day we are afraid to show ourselves, since everyone we meet tells us that there are round-ups going on.

After a fortnight in the forests, seeing no way out, I propose that we take a chance and travel to Warsaw. Several of us have acquaintances there, and perhaps we will succeed in saving ourselves. My proposal is rejected out of fear that along the way we might fall into the hands of the murderers.

Seeing that it is not possible for me to remain here, I decide to leave for Warsaw by myself. It is painful for me to take leave of my friends. Still, I start on my way. We embrace each other and express our wish that we may meet again.

After walking several kilometres I come to a village. It is evening. I enter a peasant's house. He is afraid to talk to me. He hands me a piece of bread and tells me that Warsaw is 99 kilometres away. As I stand there, I suddenly hear the sound of shooting in the distance. The peasant runs back into the house and shouts to me to run away at once. I run into the potato fields and hide there. I hear more shots. Night has fallen. Heavy rain begins to fall and continues all night. I lie there for twelve hours until dawn. I feel I will not be able get up, but with my last ounce of strength I get back on my feet. After walking a few kilometres, I see a man approaching me. By now indifferent to everything, I keep going. The man comes closer. I see from his clothes that he is a peasant and ask him the way. He thinks about it for a little while then asks me—Are you one of those who fled Treblinka?

Seeing that he feels compassion for me, I tell him that I am indeed one of those who fled and ask him for help. He tells me that he has to go to the mill to buy flour for tomorrow's holiday. But he turns back with me towards his house, some 2 kilometres away. He leads the way and I follow.

When I enter his house I see a woman with a child in her arms. I embrace the little child and kiss it. The woman looks at me in astonishment and I tell her—Dear lady, it is a whole year since I have seen a living child . . . The woman and I cry together. She gives me food, and, seeing that I am soaked through, she gives me a shirt of her husband's to put on. She mentions that it is her husband's last shirt.

I see that these people want to help me. Weeping, the woman says to me—I would very much like to help you, but I am afraid of my neighbours. After all, I have a small child . . .

After spending half an hour with them, I thank them warmly and want to say goodbye. The peasant points through the window to a barn standing in the middle of the fields not far from us. The barn belongs to a rich peasant and no one ever goes there. He advises me to hide there and come to him in the evenings, when he will give me food. I thank them and head for the barn. I burrow deep into the straw so that no one can see me. A real stroke of luck.

When evening falls I crawl out of the straw and head for my friends' house. They receive me in a very friendly fashion. After I have been sitting there for a few minutes, a neighbour suddenly enters, and without so much as saying hello slaps me hard twice on the face. He screams—Yid, come with me!

I am unfortunately helpless. The woman, seeing what he means to do to me, begs him to let go of me and allow me to escape. But he refuses to budge. The woman kisses him and begs him—Franek, what do you want from that man? Do you even know him?

He screams at her for defending me—Don't you know that these bandits set fire to Treblinka? I'll get a reward for him!

Her entreaties and weeping are in vain. Seeing that she cannot change his mind, she goes over to him, grabs him from behind and shouts to me to escape. I tear myself away and dash out of the house. I cross the garden and run a couple of hundred steps and lie down in the field. I decide not to run away from here, since it would be a shame to lose such good people. When it is clear to me that Franek has gone away, I crawl back towards my friends on all fours, go into the barn and lie down again. In the morning the peasant comes in and when he sees me he greets me warmly. He is afraid that I will be caught because the neighbours all around are very bad people. He brings me food several times a day, and in the evening I hide in the barn in the middle of the field.

I spend about two weeks in that way. Every evening I come to the house of these good people and they hand me food through the window. But one time the owner of the barn arrives and unloads some grain there. I suspect that he has seen me and therefore decide to leave my hiding place for Warsaw, come what may.

That evening I go to my friends and tell them of my decision. They try to dissuade me, out of fear that I may fall into the hands of the police patrolling the roads. But I cannot be talked out of it and say goodbye to them. The peasant tells me that the nearest railway station is Kostki, about 7 kilometres from there.

The trip is a difficult one, as the trains are full of police inspectors. Nevertheless I am able to come to Warsaw without incident, and thence to Piastow, where my friend Jarosz, a Pole, resides. At first he does not recognize me and tries to give me a handout of 5 zlotys. Then, when he realizes who I am, he is happy to see me and helps me with necessities. He also provides Aryan papers for me.

After spending several days with him, I break down morally and physically. I lose my appetite and am convinced that I have no right to be alive after all I have seen and experienced. My friends care for me and try to convince me that there are few witnesses left like me and that I need to live in order to tell it all.

Yes, I lived for a year in Treblinka under the most difficult conditions. After the revolt I wandered for two months, lived for a year as a Pole with false papers, then after the Warsaw Uprising I hid in a bunker for three and a half months until I was liberated on 17 January 1945.

Yes, I remained alive and find myself among free people. But I often ask myself why. Is it so that I might tell the world about the millions of innocent murdered victims, to be a witness to the innocent blood that was spilled by the hands of the murderers?

Yes, I remained alive to bear witness against the great slaughterhouse of Treblinka.